BREAK FREE
FROM
YOUR REINS

BREAK FREE FROM YOUR REINS

A Motivational Guide to a Greater Being

DEBORAH M. PARISE

BREAK FREE FROM YOUR REINS
A MOTIVATIONAL GUIDE TO A GREATER BEING

iUniverse books may be ordered through booksellers or by contacting:

iUniverse
1663 Liberty Drive
Bloomington, IN 47403
www.iuniverse.com
1-800-Authors (1-800-288-4677)

Because of the dynamic nature of the Internet, any web addresses or links contained in this book may have changed since publication and may no longer be valid. The views expressed in this work are solely those of the author and do not necessarily reflect the views of the publisher, and the publisher hereby disclaims any responsibility for them.

Any people depicted in stock imagery provided by Thinkstock are models, and such images are being used for illustrative purposes only. Certain stock imagery © Thinkstock.

ISBN: 978-1-4917-5567-9 (sc)
ISBN: 978-1-4917-5566-2 (hc)
ISBN: 978-1-4917-5568-6 (e)

Library of Congress Control Number: 2014921688

Print information available on the last page.

iUniverse rev. date: 04/10/2015

This book is dedicated to the people who have committed suicide.
They may be gone, but they are not forgotten.
They will forever be in our hearts.

I am filled with deep love and gratitude for my two
beautiful daughters, Chelsea Marie and Sarah Lauren,
and my precious grandson, Liam Bradley.

Children are a blessing, and life is truly a miracle.
I am here for them right here, right now, and I always will be …

Contents

Preface

How well do you know yourself? Do you know who you really are? When you are ready to put an end to the wondering and searching, and uncover the *real* you, *Break Free From Your Reins* is the perfect book for you. You will discover the true meaning of life and what you can do to live a content and peaceful life. *Break Free From Your Reins* touches on subjects many of us have questioned. A lot of people crave something in life but cannot figure out what it is. They have been searching outside of themselves for this missing link. Little do they know, all the answers are within them. They have had them all along. Consciously or unconsciously, you already know the truth about life. Psst … the key to having it all is knowing you already have it.

I am deeply honored and privileged to present to you *Break Free From Your Reins*. My intention is to provide you the enthusiasm and motivation to live a more fulfilling and gratifying lifestyle. I am overjoyed that you are spending your valuable time with me on this journey. I am confident *Break Free From Your Reins* will make a positive difference in your life.

To give you a sneak peek, you will be encouraged to break free from mind-conditioned patterns, beliefs, and self-doubt and become the extraordinary person you were put on this earth to be. You will be inspired to be confident in yourself and the choices you make. *Break Free From Your Reins* will enhance you spiritually, mentally, physically, emotionally, and socially. It provides a clear perception on life, but it is ultimately up to you to discover the true meaning. You are in charge of you and the creator of your own life.

I am profoundly grateful that I have been chosen to write *Break Free From Your Rein*. My wisdom and intuition, along with the guidance and driving energy force from a divine influence, prompted me to write *Break Free From Your Reins*. I am not a physician, therapist, counselor, or scientific expert, but I have learned well from sixty years of actual life experiences. The greatest teachers we have are our own life experiences, and every experience is knowledge. My life experiences, including the pleasant and unpleasant ones, have made me who I am today. I am the best person I can be, and I will continue to expand my knowledge to further develop into a higher existence.

I have been inspired by numerous great motivational speakers, spiritual leaders, and authors—many of whose names have been mentioned throughout this book. I have provided many of their popular, inspirational quotes in *Break Free From Your Reins*. Quotes are effective in inspiring us to achieve realization and become more aligned with the message so we can apply these practices in our everyday lives. The brilliant authors of these famous quotes have been given the appropriate acknowledgment; however, some remain anonymous. I take no credit for any of the italicized quotes included in *Break Free From Your Reins*. I have also included brief definitions of specific words being used in the book to help provide a better understanding and explanation of the words and the meaning being conveyed in the paragraphs.

To gain the most from *Break Free From Your Reins*, I encourage you to read it with an open mind, an open heart, and complete and total awareness. I will be asking you questions, but before you answer them, I want you to really examine yourself. Be honest with yourself and answer these questions truthfully. You may discover things about yourself you love, or there may be some areas where you need to improve. To get good results, you have to be able to identify your strengths and weaknesses. I, too, have benefitted from writing this book. I have discovered that putting my thoughts into words validates my beliefs. Here is what Mr. William Shakespeare said: *To thine own self be true.*"

I am confident there is something worth reading for everyone, including the younger generation. I may repeat myself at times, as all these things are interconnected. Anything I recommend in this book I have practiced, applied, lived it, and confirmed that it works. When you practice these principles on a daily basis for continued growth and development, I am confident the quality of your life will greatly improve. Please share this information with whomever you feel needs some encouragement and/or self-improvement in life. The biggest room in this world is the room for improvement.

Break Free From Your Reins is based more on the spiritual level. However, the topic of religion and a higher being is addressed. Perhaps there are some things written in here that you feel differently about. Please understand there is no offense to anyone whatsoever. These are my individual beliefs, values, and opinions I have gained through my own life experiences. You are encouraged to form your own belief system. My goal is to help guide you to living the best life possible and to encourage you to become the finest person you can be.

So there you have it. I am doing what I love best … helping others. My goal is to give back what I have received over the years. I want you to know what I know and what it takes to be happy with yourself and love life. We need to realize how incredibly blessed we are, and life is good and definitely worth living. It is time to praise and celebrate life! I extend my *love* to all of you, and I wish you *peace always*!

Introduction

Existing in this World

Are you living life to your fullest potential, or are you just existing? At times we may feel or believe that our existence does not matter in this world. Truthfully, it matters tremendously. I know for sure there are many people who are discouraged with life. I am truly affected every time I read or hear about a person committing suicide because they could no longer cope with life. Suicide is the fourth leading cause of death for adults between the ages of eighteen and sixty-five in the United States. More than thirty-eight thousand people in the United States die by suicide every year. People in today's society could definitely use more guidance, support, and love in life. We need your help. We are here to make a difference in our everyday lives and in the world. I know you want to participate in this transformation. How do I know? Because you are reading *Break Free From Your Reins*.

We are all magnificent human beings, and we have so much to contribute to this world.

We have the wisdom, creative abilities, and diverse talents to contribute to making this world a better place. We are constantly being tested by people, situations, conditions, and even our own thoughts, so we have to stay on our toes and be positive and confident that we will pass the tests. Each one of us possesses the power within to overcome adversities. There is one catch though; we have to realize it. Once we are conscious of this personal power, we will be unstoppable.

There are many attractive, wealthy, successful people in this world, and we tend to compare ourselves to them, but we were purposely created uniquely with different intentions in life. We are not ordinary; we are extraordinary. When we become aware of our thoughts, words, and actions, we have the potential to impact the world in a positive way. The possibilities are endless. What brings you enjoyment might be another person's weakness. The people you admire were once inspired by other people to become who they are today. I am sure you have already been a positive influence in someone's life. A simple act of kindness can make a big difference.

Every single person has a purpose and something good and of value to contribute to the world, regardless of a person's status. The criminals in jail, the homeless on the streets, drug addicts, alcoholics, doctors, lawyers, teachers, pastors, entrepreneurs, etc., all have access to the divine power within them to become the person they are meant to be. Ultimately, it is up to each individual to realize this and have the will to do so. You have been given a gift, the breath of life. It is up to you to love it, nourish it, enrich it, and live it!

Break Free From Your Reins is part of my evolution and divine purpose in life. I have been empowered and driven to write and share this book to inspire you to view life in a more positive manner. I assure you that your existence is also part of the divine intention of this world. You are capable of fulfilling your purpose in life and living the best life ever.

Personal Testimony

At one point in life, I was searching for answers and contentment. I wanted to know the truth about life. I would ask myself who am I, what am I doing here, where am I going, who and what should I believe, etc. I became passionate about finding the answers. This is the testimony behind my transformation. I love to tell my story, because it is incredible.

My mother and father were wonderful parents to me. I was baptized in a Catholic church and raised as a Christian and to believe in God. As I got older, I did not know for sure if I truly did believe in God. I struggled with this thought for a very long time. I would get mad at God, because I never understood why God would allow bad things to happen. (As you read more, you will come to understand why God intends for these things to happen.) I felt lost, like there was something missing in my life. I explored other religions. I prayed for answers and guidance from whomever or whatever, until something phenomenal happened.

One evening, I was home alone, lying on the chaise, and I was on the verge of falling asleep. Suddenly, out of nowhere, came a soft gentle voice that whispered in my ear and asked me this simple question: "What do you want?" I immediately replied (in my mind), *I want to be happy*. Normally, an experience like this would frighten me, but it was a very comforting feeling. This was the turning point that changed my life. I felt I had what is called a *spiritual encounter*. You see, when you want something badly enough, it will happen. Since that night, I have felt a sense of mental calmness, and I know that everything is going to be just fine. I know in my heart that a higher power truly exists and that I am loved. This I know for sure. After that experience, things started happening like a domino effect.

My Inspirations

I loved watching the *Oprah Winfrey Show* because I always learned something new. As soon as I would get home from work, I would tune into her show. One day, I was watching a segment about *The Secret*. Her guests were talking about the law of attraction. I became so engrossed in their conversation and I began to relate to what they were saying. I suddenly had an epiphany or an *aha* moment. One could say this is when spirit recognizes spirit. This realization was so compelling; I instantly understood what they were talking about from a new and deeper perspective. I was anxious to start practicing this theory and create the life I wanted. I was so excited I recall telling my youngest daughter, Sarah, and her friend about the law of attraction and how we can attract what we want through our thoughts. I wanted to tell the whole world about it!

Soon after that show, I was watching another episode, when Ms. Winfrey was talking about Mr. Eckhart Tolle's book titled *A New Earth—Awakening to Your Life's Purpose*. She went on and on about it and highly recommended that everyone read it. It was included in her book club, and I was eager to read it. Mr. Tolle is known as the most spiritually influential person in the world. I participated in Ms. Winfrey's and Mr. Tolle's webinar class based on *A New Earth*. Mr. Tolle provided practical teachings for waking up to a new, enlightened mind-set, and seeking a more loving self and a more loving planet. Wow, what a team! Ms. Winfrey and Mr. Tolle have been a true inspiration to me. I am bowing to you both in gratitude. Namasté. I became passionate about spirituality and the law of attraction and decided my intention in life is to enlighten everyone about these best life practices. I know for sure we were put on this earth to help each other.

A New Earth is the most inspirational book I have ever read. It provided the tools I needed to begin my transformation. This is when I began to see the light. In some cases, people have to reach the lowest point of despair or desperation in life before having an experience like this. Letting go of an attachment or an obsession can also wake people up. This progression is often called enlightenment or an awakening.

I highly recommend several of Mr. Tolle's books, along with other useful books written by many well-known spiritual teachers. Their words of wisdom have inspired me to be more and do what I am called to do. My mission in life is to help you do the same. I invite you to check out the list of sources I have provided in the back for your convenience.

CHAPTER 1

Living a Meaningful Life

Are you totally confused about life in general? Are you struggling with your thoughts? Are you angry? Is there a lot of drama in your life? Are you under a lot of peer pressure? Are you or your parents divorced? Do you feel overweight? Do you feel insecure about yourself? Are you going through a breakup? Do you feel like your world is falling apart?

Or just maybe … you have it all together and life is going great but you could use a little more reassurance and guidance on subjects you are uncertain about. American businessman Mr. John D. Rockefeller once said, *"Don't be afraid to give up the good to go for the great."*[1]

I completely understand what you may be going through right now and what your perspective on life may be. My goal is to shed some light on subjects that might have never crossed your mind. You have to understand that there is more to life than meets the eye. You are loved and surrounded by many supporters. I am one of them. Very few of us make it through life without some kind of assistance. You are a wonderful, competent person with great potential, but

---

[1] BrainyQuote.com, accessed August 14, 2014, http://www.brainyquote.com/quotes/quotes/j/johndrock119902.html

sometimes our own thoughts deceive us. I am telling you that you are very capable of living a more fulfilling life.

I bet you are totally exhausted from trying to be someone you were never meant to be. Guess what … you are not alone. I have been there and done that. At one time, I was obsessed with my appearance and what other people thought about me. I wanted to be absolutely perfect and beautiful so that everyone would like me. I was constantly seeking approval from others instead of believing in myself. I truly felt like I was not good enough. Why? I cannot tell you why or when I became that way, but I can assure you that I was not happy. I was so tired of trying to be someone other than who I was created to be. I was living life as an imposter and that is definitely not the way to exist. I was living life according to someone else's expectations and wanting to be someone other than myself. I never thought about *me* and what made *me* happy. No wonder I was miserable a lot of the time. I was resisting my own true self and was going against the flow of life. I did not realize that I was already beautiful inside and out and made exactly the way I was supposed to be. The good news is I have come to love and appreciate who I am. Why in the world would I want to be someone else? I am letting go of self-doubt, all limitations, and all the old stuff. I am returning to the original state I was born into. I am revealing this imposter and making it official. Would the real Deborah Marie Parise please stand up? Here I am. It is the real me. I am so happy to meet me and finally be me. I strongly encourage you to do the same and be the real you. You will feel much relief when the mask finally comes off, and you can be your natural, beautiful self.

First and foremost, I want everyone in this world to be happy. Can you imagine that? It affects me every time I see someone who is sad and struggling with life. I have to remind you that life is really good and is not what you may *think* it is. This is what I know for sure through my actual life experiences. Life is our greatest teacher. From these experiences, I have a more meaningful life and a greater understanding about *us* in the most undeniable way. Here is an amazing quote written by a musician named Mr. Arthur Rubinstein: *"I have found that if you love life, life will love you back."*[2]

So here is the deal: to improve your life, you have to be willing to accept and apply the wisdom and knowledge offered to you right here in *Break Free From Your Reins*. I have tested the waters, and I highly encourage you to see for yourself. I know it will impact your life in a positive way. You already have what it takes to achieve inner peace and contentment, but you have to find out for yourself. When you are comfortable with differences and keep an open mind and become enthusiastic about change, you will live a purpose-driven life. You also have to be willing to give it your all. It is your choice. I love, honor, and respect you, whatever you choose to do.

Thank you so much for taking this journey with me. You are going to be surprised when you discover how simple and wonderful life can be. You are on the right track to living a better life. I appreciate your willingness to be open to new ideas and beliefs. I am extremely excited that you are ready to accept this challenge. When your intentions are aligned with the source of all creation, I know for sure that you can create the life you desire. You are well-equipped to take charge of your life. *You* and only *you* are responsible for it. Life is precious. Take care of it, nurture it, improve it, and love it!

Parents/Legal Guardians

Are you constantly being hassled by your parents, grandparents, legal guardians, or whoever is raising you? I am going to refer to them as parents, but you may identify her/him/them to your situation or liking. Getting back to my question. Are your parents nagging you all the time about homework, cleaning your room, your appearance, who you are hanging out with, and so on? Do they try to control every single thing you attempt to do, even if you are an adult and old enough to make your own decisions?

---

2   BrainyQuote.com, accessed August 14, 2014, http://www.brainyquote.com/quotes/quotes/a/arthurrubi104208.html

Well ... I am here to reassure you that your parents love you and are concerned about your well-being. They may not always tell you or show you, but they do. Some parents have difficulty expressing their love and affection toward their children for various reasons. It could be that their parents never showed them love. Why? Because many parents are still trying to figure out what life is all about. If this is the case, how can we expect them to know all the right answers when they do not know themselves? We depend on our parents to guide and protect us and teach us everything they know. We should still love and respect them anyway.

Understand that we are products of our upbringings. In most life situations, parents pass on to their children what they learned from their parents, and so on. It is difficult to break free from the mind-conditioned patterns, traditions, and old habits they acquired from their parents.

However, there are exceptions where they may have gone in another direction and developed from being in different conditions or circumstances.

Society and egos can easily influence a person's behavior. Some people think that self-worth or value comes from what we *do* to succeed in life as opposed to who we *are*. Many parents get caught up in their careers and trying to keep up with the lifestyles of others. Coping with the demands and pressures of everyday life can be stressful. Parents can quickly become unaware of their behavior in the home. Their words, emotions, and expectations can get out of control. They do not realize their children are observing them closely as they perform daily routine responsibilities as an adult and parent. This is why we have emotionally dysfunctional families. I have to tell you that you may have picked up some of your parents' habits, which they, too, unconsciously acquired from their parents. Some may be good, some may be bad. A habit is an acquired behavior pattern regularly followed until it has become almost involuntary.

Bad habits can be smoking cigarettes, drinking alcohol excessively, smoking marijuana, abusing drugs, etc. Bad habits can also include inappropriate behavior such as arguing, shouting, swearing, lying, etc. Worrying, complaining, and doubting are bad habits you may have learned from them. There are plenty out there, but it is okay because you can actively choose to change and break those habits.

On the other hand, you may be experiencing a happy and peaceful lifestyle already. Your parents probably came from a loving and harmonious family and, therefore, have provided the same type of environment for you. They certainly should be praised for being good role models. Your parents were probably very aware of their behavior and made wise choices. They taught from their hearts and from what they know to be true and understood the importance of life. You have witnessed their good behavioral habits and are already on the right track with your life. You can now be the "conscious" parent and set a good example for your children. You will provide a good foundation and beginning for your children.

Now in some cases, the roles are reversed in a home, and an older child is actually caring for the parent(s) and maybe siblings too. If the parent(s) are alcoholics, drug addicts, disabled, etc., someone is automatically thrown into this role by being responsible for those living there and the daily household operations. When you are in charge at home, you must be the role model for the others. Although it may be a tough road to follow, remain strong and remember that God never gives you more than you can handle. Keep the positive energy flowing by consistently doing what is right. You will be the one they admire and look up to. You will make a difference in their lives and this world. I highly commend those of you who are currently in this situation.

At one time, your parents were attracted to each other, and you were conceived. If your parents are divorced or separated, it does not mean your life is over. You cannot use that as an excuse, because you have choices too. You can choose to accept the situation as it is and make the most of it (this is what I recommend you do), or you can choose to be angry about it and be unhappy. Your life can be as happy as you choose to make it, so the next time you are with one or both parents, be considerate and enjoy the time you spend with them. Do not play the blame game. It is a waste of energy and will not resolve anything. They may be still struggling with life and are doing their best from what *they* know. We must accept them for whom they are and love them right back!

If things are not working for you these days, and you know you are on the wrong path, what can you do? You have the choice to *change*, no matter what the circumstances may be. It is all up to you. You can grow beyond whatever you are currently experiencing. Now is the perfect time to break free from your reins and take full responsibility for your life, on your own terms and conditions. You were designed to develop your own personal ideas and beliefs. You have to be willing to let go of certain beliefs and customs you have learned during your childhood that represent your parents' views. It is time for you to live your life according to what you believe and trust your intuition. It will take practice to break the old habits and patterns. Be mindful of the choices you make, because they will impact your life one way or another. You will learn and evolve from both right and wrong choices. It is not what we know that makes us who we are; it is the decisions we make. Believe what *your* heart tells you, and write your own story.

Children

Some of you may be fathers, mothers, step-parents, or legal guardians to a child. Be grateful, because a child is a blessing from God. A child is a precious being of this world and requires a lot of love and nurturing from the very beginning. There is much responsibility that comes with raising a child. A child is totally dependent upon his or her parents for everything during the early stages of life. Be a loving and devoted parent. The most valuable gift you can give your child (or anyone, for that matter) is your time. Soon your child will be grown, and one of the hardest things for a parent to do is to let go of the child. We as parents have to let go of the role of "I know what is best for you." By giving your child roots and wings, you will be proud to let your child become his or her own person. Here are some words of wisdom from the book *The Prophet* by Mr. Kahlil Gibran: *"Your children are not your children. They are the sons and daughters of life's longing for itself. They came through you but not from you and though they are with you yet they belong not to you."*[3]

It is beneficial for children to have both a loving male and female presence in their lives. Each parent possesses many fine qualities to contribute to raising a child. One may affect his or her child in such a way that makes the child be better, while the other parent may not have this to offer. For the parents who are living separately, the child should still be included in both their lives. Having the love, help, and guidance from two parents can provide a more stable beginning for a child to grow into adulthood.

The first five years of a child's life are the most important. Children watch every move their parents make. They learn from observing, listening, and following everything their parents say, do, and believe. As parents, we cannot act foolishly and then expect our children to grow up being perfectly normal. Parents must be on their best behavior at all times, especially during those first five years. Children are like sponges. They absorb everything they see and hear, good and bad. The best technique to use when teaching a child good behavior is for you to *be* the role model for your child. Lead by example. Be the best you can be to set a good example for your child. Your child will grow up being the best he or she can be. Please do not be the parent who says, "Do as I say and not as I do."

Children can certainly test our patience. When a child throws a tantrum, we should settle them down, hold them, hug them, and tell them you love them. They are growing and learning and get

---

[3] Kahlil Gibran, *The Prophet*, the section on children, Juan Cole's personal website, accessed June 12, 2014, http://www-personal.umich.edu/~jrcole/gibran/prophet/prophet.htm

easily frustrated especially when they cannot do something. They should not be punished for that. When you raise your hand to a child, you are teaching them that violence and hostility is acceptable. Discipline them in a different way or divert their attention to something else. When we use a calming method to help them deal with their frustrations, they quickly resume normal behavior. Most importantly, when we do not react to their poor behavior, they know *you* are the one in control.

From another standpoint, children can actually be our spiritual teachers. Some essential life lessons we can learn from them are: (1) how to be happy, because if you will notice, a child is usually happy for no reason; (2) how to always succeed in getting what one wants; (3) how to stay busy like a bee; and (4) how to love, trust, and have faith, because they put their total faith and trust in us as parents and love us no matter what. The next time you are in the presence of a child, observe him or her closely for a little while and you will see what I mean. Children love unconditionally and live life to the fullest. They are simply amazing!

Yes, I am a parent, and I have been guilty of making poor choices. I could have used some help along my journey, especially with controlling my thoughts and emotions during my younger years. I must admit I could have practiced better parenting skills and more patience when raising my daughters. I am very grateful (thank you Marty) that I was able to stay home from work for eight years and care for my children. I loved being a stay-at-home mom.

However, this is today, and I am truly blessed and grateful that I now know what it takes to be a good role model. I am practicing on my wonderful little grandson, who I adore. When we are together, I am fully in the present moment. I am more patient with him than I ever was with my daughters. I realize that he is exploring life and curious about everything. He asks me so many questions, and I answer them to the best of my ability, even if he asks over and over again, "Why, Grammie?" I told him he is my little guru, but he said, "No. I am Liam." I love that little boy with all my being.

I have learned so much about life and will continue to seek ways to become better. I am purposely passing this wisdom and knowledge on to my daughters, grandson, nieces, and anyone who is destined to read it. I am confident *Break Free From Your Reins* will change people's lives for the better.

Note: It is everyone's responsibility to report suspected child abuse or neglect to the proper authorities in order to protect the safety of a child (younger than eighteen years). Please refer to the National Organizations section of Child Welfare Information Gateway that offers information about child welfare at: http://www.childwelfare.gov/organizations/index.cfm. It only takes a moment to make a difference in a child's life.

Take Charge

If you knew today was your last day alive, what would you do, who would you spend it with, and where would you go? Take advantage of the 86,400 seconds provided to you every day. Appreciate life and all it has to offer. Live each day as if it was your last. So what are you going to do with this precious gift?

Chapter 2

Connecting with the Source

We are entitled to our own opinions and beliefs. I respect whatever you believe regarding the formation or beginning of human life. This is what I have figured out over the years. All that exists (the entire universe and all that is living) was created by a divine source or entity. Hence, all living forms are connected to this divine source or power. We were born into this world as unconditioned human beings. You are physically here, and there is no denying that. As human beings, we are connected to each other through this powerful source. Our minds and physical parts may differ, but our inner beings are the same. Our inner beings are what connect us to the source that supplies us with the "recipe" for life.

There are a variety of words or labels we use to identify the source from which we were created. It could be referred to as a religion, a scientific theory or process, a philosophic concept, or simply a way of life. Names associated with these concepts may include: Adonai, Allah, the Big Bang Theory, Buddha, Creator, Divine, Elohim, God, Great Architect of the Universe, Heavenly Father, Highest Power, Holy Spirit, Jehovah, King of Kings, Lord of Lords, Messiah, Prophet, Supreme Being, Universal Intelligence, Yahweh, etc. If whomever or whatever you call the source, entity, process, etc. from which you originated is not listed, please add the name or word(s) to the list. But answer this one question: does it really matter what we label our source?

When we lose connection to the source of all creation, we feel lost and separate, and we may feel as though something died within us. No worries, because the good news is we always have the choice to restore our connection. We all have the opportunity to reconnect at any time, but we must choose to. We can reconnect by speaking, listening, praying, and meditating (this is explained later in the book). The source will always be there to provide the love, guidance, and support we need. When we do not listen or follow that guidance, we will feel discouraged and experience fear. Stay connected. It is that simple!

I have a very strong and direct connection to the source. Without this connection, I truly cannot do it on my own because I have tried. I can say I now have peace and contentment in life. I receive guidance from the source during meditation and stillness. I express gratitude every day for the blessings bestowed upon me. I am deeply honored that I have been called by this divine source to write *Break Free From Your Reins*. I am confident it will provide you the knowledge and empowerment to become a better human being.

Beliefs

During life, you will have to make many decisions and choices on who and what to believe. A belief is a thought you give power by making it real or accepting it as true. Do you believe there is a "God?" Wikipedia provides, *"For the general concept of "a god", see Deity."* I clicked on *"Deity,"* and this is just the first paragraph of the full content provided: *"In religious belief, a deity is a supernatural being, who may be thought of as holy, divine, or sacred. Some religions have one supreme deity, others have multiple deities of various ranks."*[4] People usually want evidence before they will believe something.

---

[4]   *Wikipedia*, s.v. "Deity," last modified June 5, 2014, http://en.wikipedia. org/wiki/Diety

Nonbelievers may ask, "How can you believe in something or someone that cannot be seen by the human eye?" Wikipedia states, *"Atheism is, in a broad sense, the rejection of belief in the existence of deities."*[5] Believers may justify their faith in something that is invisible by the wind. You know it is there, because you can feel it and see things moving. Gas is invisible, but you can smell it. You cannot see music, but you can hear it. The thoughts that occur in our minds are invisible too.

There are so many beliefs in this world and what you believe is your own private, personal business. You should feel confident with your beliefs regarding the creation of the universe and the human race. If you are still uncertain, research and explore other beliefs or religions. You may not believe all of their exact teachings, but you can figure out which one is best for you. No matter what, I value you as an individual for whatever you believe or do not believe.

I personally choose to believe there is single master creator who I refer to as *God*. I strongly believe God created me and the totality of the universe. I believe God is the provider of knowledge, truth, and light. Since the vast majority of us use the word *God* as our creator, I am going to use God throughout this book. If you have a different label for your creator, replace the word God with the name, word(s), or phrase you use for your belief system. Please use whatever works for *you*. I want you to feel totally comfortable with reading *Break Free From Your Reins*.

At one point in life, I had many questions and doubts about my beliefs and religion. In my mind, I said I believed in God, but did I really? I felt I was a good and decent person, but did I practice what God preached? I can tell you one thing: I desperately wanted my life to change, because I was not happy. I have always had a desire to please other people, but I finally realized I should be pleasing God and myself most importantly. Once I started "being" the person

5   *Wikipedia*, s.v. "Atheism," last modified June 6, 2014, http://en.wikipedia.org/wiki/Atheism

God created me to be, my life suddenly began to transform. Things started happening effortlessly for me. This was proof enough for me to believe that an all-powerful divine entity truly does exist. I am evolving into a higher consciousness, and I am more aware of my thoughts, words, emotions, and actions. This awareness helps me to make better choices, and I am more content and at peace with myself and life. I am so overwhelmed with gratitude that at times I cry tears of joy.

Since we were created by God (remember to replace this word with what you believe), we are all one and connected (as children) through God. None of us are separate from God. God is the source to all love, all power, all supply, and all life. Pay attention to the next sentence. If God created each and every one of us, then we all have God's power within us, similar to how we have inherited our parents' genetics. Wherever we are and whatever we are doing, we have access to this Godlike power. With this power, we have the ability to reach our highest potential and achieve great things. Whenever you feel lost or have the need for support and guidance, you have a direct connection to God 24 hours a day, 7 days a week (24/7). God is always right there for you, within you, and ready and waiting to help you.

Do you remember the game show *Who Wants to Be a Millionaire?* When the contestant did not know the answer to a question, he or she could resort to using a lifeline. This meant they could call a person they depended on for the answer. In some cases, that person did not provide the correct answer. The point I would like to make here is that God is your lifeline and available for you 24/7. The difference between the game show and God is that you can definitely rely on God for all the right answers.

Religion

Being part of a collective group of people and practicing specific customs or rituals should be a positive experience. Organized religions can be a great support structure, and many offer good, educational programs. Are you confident about the religion you support? You should not feel pressured into going to church (or whatever you call your place of worship), because you will miss the message. Go to church only if you feel good about going. If you do not agree with a specific belief structure, check out other religious organizations. Do not feel obligated to belong to the same religion in which you were raised. Follow your own path and beliefs, and break free from your reins.

Going to church helps me to stay on the right path. I used to attend Catholic mass on a regular basis, but I felt a need to expand my knowledge. I decided to explore other religions to determine which one conformed to my beliefs. A while ago, my girlfriend attended Jehovah's Witnesses meetings, so I decided to tag along to see what they practiced. I have recently been attending a nondenominational Christian service. Nondenominational Christian institutions are not formally aligned with an established religious denomination. Their practice provides spiritual growth through practical Bible-based teachings and many other great programs. Each week, the pastor selects different verses from the Bible and fully explains their significance in life and then provides examples for members to better understand the teaching. Since the language in the Bible is difficult for me to understand, this is exactly what I need. I can relate to the messages being conveyed. Contemporary Christian music is performed live on stage during the services and worship nights. The music is phenomenal and has a direct effect on my soul. I am open-minded about new ideas and practices, and I also enjoy interacting with people who have the same moral values and beliefs as I have. Going to this church is a rewarding experience for *me*.

For *me*, my main focus is on my relationship with God. What my own spiritual intuition tells me is far greater than following someone else's beliefs and thought process. I know right from wrong. When I make the right choices and do the right thing, I will always have peace in my heart. I can meditate or pray to connect with God anywhere. It does not necessarily have to be in a church, synagogue, mosque, sanctuary, temple, Kingdom Hall, chapel, etc.

I am a US citizen, and as it declares in the Pledge of Allegiance, we are *one nation under God.* We need to realize that we are truly wonderful human beings regardless of our beliefs (e.g., atheists, agnostics, Buddhists, Christians, Hindus, Jews, Muslims, Mormons, etc.).

We are in this lifetime together. Let us come together and make the best of life. Let us make things right with ourselves. Let us learn to forgive and help and support each other. Let us be grateful and appreciate everyone for who they are. Let us put God first, and love and honor God with all our might. Let us unite spiritually and grow to be the finest human beings we can possibly be. This is what President Abraham Lincoln once said: *"When I do good, I feel good. When I do bad, I feel bad. That's my religion."*

The Bible

Many people read and follow the Bible. Here is the definition directly from Wikipedia:

> *The Bible (from Koine Greek τὰ βιβλία, tà biblía, "the books") is a canonical collection of texts considered sacred in Judaism and Christianity. There is no single "Bible" and many Bibles with varying contents exist. The term Bible is shared between Judaism and Christianity, although the contents of each of their collections of canonical texts is not the same. Different religious groups include different books within their Biblical canons, in different orders, and sometimes divide or combine books, or incorporate additional material into canonical books.*
>
> *The Bible is widely considered to be the best selling book of all time, has estimated annual sales of 100*

> *million copies, and has been a major influence on literature and history, especially in the West where it was the first mass-printed book.*[6]

Is the Bible literal (factual, truthful, and exact), or is it allegory (symbol, metaphor, or story)? If the Bible was written and rewritten several times by select groups of individuals and their interpretation of how we should live life, do we know for sure if everything was translated correctly? People do not always hear and see things the same way as others do. One person's interpretation can be quite different from another's.

I once took a communication class, and we did an exercise on conveying information. A large group of students sat in a circle, and the professor started out by whispering a message into one student's ear. That student was supposed to repeat the exact same words he or she heard from the professor to the next person, and so on. This process continued until it came to the very last person in the circle. Do you think he or she heard exactly what the professor said at the beginning? This is an excellent example of what I am explaining above.

The Bible was written in a language that is hard for many people to understand. There is nothing difficult to understand about believing in God and being an honorable person by doing the right thing. That, my friends, is basically what the Bible teaches us. You may ask, "What is the right thing?" Start by reading and following the ten fundamental rules to live a righteous life. These rules are known as the Ten Commandments in the Bible. The Ten Commandments relate to ethics and worship and teach us how to apply love in every aspect of life. When you disobey God's rules, you will feel broken. Sadly, we have all broken these rules, but we always

---

[6]   *Wikipedia*, s.v. "Bible," last modified June 7, 2014, http://en.wikipedia. org/wiki/Bible

have the choice to humble ourselves, ask for forgiveness, and begin again with a new perspective on life.

There are many excellent Bible verses that are probably accurate, but we also have the spirit of truth and wisdom of life within us. This wisdom (also known as intuition) is our Godlike power. We were born with it and have access to it at any time. When I am faced with a difficult situation, I connect with God personally to get the guidance and answers I need. Many people do not use this power, because maybe they are unaware of it or even fear it and end up searching for answers elsewhere. Yes, there are many great leaders, books, resources, etc., that put you on the right path and provide you the information you need, but ultimately, you have to have confidence in yourself. Connect with God and follow your own intuition. You will have perfect peace, and good things will happen in your life.

Faith

Faith is a very deep trust, belief, and confidence in something or someone that does not rely on proof of evidence. Faith is being certain of what you do not see. Although God is invisible to us, we have to have faith in our creator. God created us, and we have an unlimited supply of power rooted within us. This power goes far beyond the thinking mind and provides the strength and drive for us to achieve great things. We have the capability to be anything we desire, as long as we have faith and trust in God. Have you ever heard this saying: "If you have faith as big as a mustard seed, you can move a mountain?" With God, anything is possible. There are no limitations.

Since you have this inner presence or power within you, you must also have faith in yourself. Believe in yourself, your intuition, and your individual abilities. We are all artists; use your imagination, be productive, and do something creative. Take photographs, paint pictures, make jewelry, build furniture, design a website, play an instrument, grow a garden, design clothing, etc. Do something you enjoy, because it makes life more fun and exciting. You could probably spend hours upon hours doing what you love to do, and it will not seem like work.

Whenever you are unsure about anything, ask God for guidance. God is always there for you and will guide you in the right direction. You will get certain signs from God—some good, some not so good—but you have to have faith in God and be conscious at all times so that you are aware of these signs. You will get warning signs indicating that perhaps it is time to make some positive changes in your life. A friend of mine calls it getting "the tap." When you ignore the tap, the tap will get stronger until you do what God is guiding you to do. A headache could be a sign of stress and to slow down and simplify your life. You will get signs of encouragement on *who* to contact, *what* to say or do, *where* to go, *why* it may be happening, and *when* to act upon a feeling. God will also give you signs that indicate you are on the right track and doing a great job, such as getting a promotion. I know one thing for sure: when I do the right thing and follow the right path, everything seems to go my way.

There are people who believe signs to be coincidences. They believe they are functions of the brain that select from numerous objects in the world that fit the story someone is telling them. Some others believe the signs indicate a non-physical energy source like perhaps a spirit guide or angel is attempting to communicate with them. It is okay to break the formality of things and be a little less intense. I have more of a lighthearted attitude. I certainly appreciate life, and I also like to have fun. It appears to me that these signs are coming from God to build our faith. To me, they indicate that I am being spiritually uplifted, and that my life is becoming more balanced and in alignment with God.

Here is one of my stories about feathers. I really enjoy walking outdoors any chance I get. Suddenly, it seemed like every time I walked, I would find a feather lying on the ground. I have a collection of them at home and at work. Something as simple as a feather could be an indication that the universe is communicating directly with me. Another interpretation of seeing a feather is that I am receiving absolute reassurance that everything is as it should be. If I had not been in a conscious state, I would have probably walked right by the feathers without even noticing them.

Signs could come in the form of numbers. I have been seeing the numbers 1111 or 111. I see them on clocks, register receipts, my cell phone, billboards, etc. I see them everywhere. Once I stopped at a gas station, and I saw a huge sign in the parking lot with 1111 written on it. I had to take a picture of it with my cell phone. I get a good feeling when I see this specific number, because I think it could be a sign of a spiritual awakening. I have read that 1111 is an indication that a shift is happening in the world of increased awareness, and it is changing for the better. I have heard people say that when you see particular numbers or three numbers alike in a row, you are supposed to make a wish. Instead of wishing for something, I usually thank God at that moment for all my blessings. I cannot help but smile to myself when I am given a sign. I get a calm, peaceful, and secure feeling like I am being guided and protected.

Always enjoy and cherish each and every precious moment, whether it is good or not so good. God is your strength in good times and in bad. It is evident when things are good, but keep that in mind when life seems difficult. There are really no bad moments in our lives, but we *think* so at the time. We experience emotional distress not from the actual situation but from our thoughts about it. Sometimes we can make mountains out of mole hills.

We have to remember that God is always working to make things right in this world. We have to have faith during the desperate moments and trying times. Even when you feel like you cannot go on, reach out to God. I know it can be particularly hard after the loss of a loved one or a divorce. Take time for the healing process, but we have to bounce back. Please keep in mind that it was time for this situation to occur, and accept it as it is. It could be time for someone to physically leave this world because of age or for reasons beyond our knowing. It could be that the divorce was for the better for the couple involved. We may come to find out the reasons for these occurrences later in life, or we may never know. Either way, we must take on life's challenges, and keep the faith and trust in our wonderful creator.

I came across a very inspirational quote that I live by every day, and I am sharing it with you. The name of the author is Mr. Rick Warren, and it was written using the word *God*. I like it so much and want to share it with you. For those of you who call your creator something other than God, please replace that word with whatever fits your beliefs. It goes like this:

> *Happy Moments—Praise God;*
> *Difficult Moments—Seek God;*
> *Quiet Moments—Worship God;*
> *Painful Moments—Trust God;*
> *Every Moment—Thank God.[7]*

Spirituality

So we talked a little bit about different beliefs in the previous section, but do you know what spirituality is? I researched the word on the Internet and have provided the definition from Wikipedia for you:

> *Traditionally spirituality has been defined as a process of personal transformation in accordance with religious ideals. Since the 19th century spirituality is often separated from religion, and has become more oriented on subjective experience and psychological growth. It may refer to almost any kind of meaningful*

[7]   "Rick Warren > Quotes > Quotable Quote," Goodreads.com, accessed August 15, 2014, https://www.goodreads.com/quotes/419680-happy-moments-praise-god-difficult-moments-seek-god-quiet-moments

activity or blissful experience, but without a single, widely-agreed definition.

Modern spirituality is centered on the "deepest values and meanings by which people live." It embraces the idea of an ultimate or an alleged immaterial reality. It envisions an inner path enabling a person to discover the essence of his/her being.[8]

In other words, spirituality exists when you experience a deeper meaning to life and discover your true identity. Spirituality is having your own experiences and beliefs and fulfilling your purpose for existence. There is no particular belief structure in place or a formality (rituals) to follow like there is in a specific religion. You practice someone else's beliefs in a religion.

My definition of spirituality is when we become aware of our spiritual essence, and we experience a greater alertness and aliveness within ourselves. Spirituality is the practice of connecting and aligning our inner most being with a divine power greater than ourselves. We become connected in such a way that we allow this greater power to guide us in life. When we consistently practice spirituality, we will develop a deeper connection with our source and the better we will become. The more aligned we are, the less pain and suffering we will experience. We will grow spiritually when we choose love over fear during the tough times.

You can certainly practice spirituality while belonging to an organized religion. It will not interfere with your religion. In fact, it will actually enhance your religious beliefs. God is the source of spiritual life. Spirituality and religion are both valuable in strengthening your belief in God, believing in yourself, and evolving

---

[8] *Wikipedia*, s.v. "Spirituality," last modified June 5, 2014, http://en.wikipedia.org/wiki/Spirituality

into a greater being. Explore what best suits your needs, stay open-minded, and accept others for what they believe as well.

We are all spiritual entities living on this earth in physical form. Our entire beings, including our mental, physical, and social beings, are completely dependent upon our spiritual beings. The core of spirituality is knowing yourself and discovering "the inner being," or the very essence, within you that is deeper than the mind and the constant excessive stream of thoughts.

Spiritual growth is when you want to enrich your life and learn to be more conscious of your thoughts and behavior, you provide more value, and you are ready to help and encourage other people to do the same. Be a part of the ripple effect and spread your light all over the place. There are many people who are struggling with life. Reach out to them, offer your support, be the inspiration for them. They may need a little encouragement, and it might be just enough to make a huge impact in their lives. I am where I am today from being inspired and motivated by many wonderful people. Be the positive influence for someone today and keep the ripple effect going.

Break Free From Your Reins is part of my life's purpose. My intention is to help myself, along with the people of this world, to evolve and grow spiritually. I highly encourage everyone to practice spirituality. Together, we will prove our unwavering determination for more peace, love, and unity in this world.

Miracles

Do you believe in miracles? Life is a miracle. I get all excited because I know miracles happen every day. I have experienced them for myself. Here is the definition of the word *miracle* from Dictionary.com: *"an effect or extraordinary event in the physical world that surpasses all known human natural powers and is ascribed to a supernatural cause; such an effect or event manifesting or considered as a work of God."*[9]

---

[9]   *Dictionary.com*, s.v. "miracle," accessed June 12, 2014, http://dictionary. reference.com/browse/miracle?s=t&path=/

A miracle is a sudden positive energy force that occurs which can be unexpected and unexplainable. Some people believe a miracle is an occurrence that requires a higher power (other than ourselves) to accomplish the work. In spite of this, we (human beings) are actually capable of making miracles happen. The source is through the power of God within us. It does not matter whether we are asking for something small or something grand. God works wonders for us and through us to bring about these miracles.

Miracles happen by simply having a positive frame of mind. Changing our thoughts, attitudes, and outlook will bring about miracles. Desiring something simple and minute, such as a close parking spot, finding something you have lost, or a phone call can happen with the right approach. These small requests are still considered miracles. When we believe wholeheartedly that God will answer our requests, anything is possible. Do you know there have been people diagnosed with incurable diseases or illnesses that have survived and are completely healed and still living today? You have the power and strength to overcome any difficulty. You have to assume the feeling that you are going to be all right, and let positive thoughts and emotions consume you. You have to become the healing power.

Here is a true miracle story. A newborn baby, Jamie Ogg, was pronounced dead at birth by doctors. The mother, however, noticed her son had started making slight movements while she was holding him. The baby's doctor explained to the parents that these movements were reflexive and not a sign of life. The mother said, *"We'd resigned ourselves to the fact that we were going to lose him, and we were just trying to make the most of those last, precious moments."*[10] The baby's mother would not give up hope. She continued to love him and cradle him anyway, and the miracle happened. Little Jamie

---

[10] "Mom's hug revives baby that was pronounced dead," Today Parenting, accessed June 12, 2014, http://today.msnbc. msn.com/id/38988444/ns/today-parenting and family/t/ moms-hug-revives-baby-was-pronounced-dead/

opened his eyes for the first time. She had the loving energy force within her to revive her son and bring him back to life. Jamie Ogg is alive and doing well today in Sydney, Australia.

A miracle is to witness the natural birth of a baby or puppies, kittens, or any kind of animal being born into the world. Flowers blooming, plants growing, the sun and moon shining, and the rain and snow coming down from the sky are all miracles too. Look for the miracles, because they are all around and always happening.

Dr. Albert Einstein believed in miracles. This is what he wrote: *"There are only two ways to live your life. One is as though nothing is a miracle. The other is as though everything is a miracle."*[11]

---

[11] "Albert Einstein > Quotes > Quotable Quote," Goodreads. com, accessed August 15, 2014, http://www.goodreads.com/ quotes/987-there-are-only-two-ways-to-live-your-life-one

Chapter 3

Understanding Your Mind and Thoughts

Thoughts

Your mind is the psychological form of who you are. Basically, your mind enables you to be conscious, think, feel, remember, reason, perceive, imagine, etc. Do you know your thoughts create your life? Your natural state of being vibrates at a frequency. When you give a thought attention, more thoughts will join in at the same frequency level. It will become stronger, and soon you will be attracting equal vibration. Every thought you have either lowers or raises your vibration. Your vibration will be at a higher frequency when you have positive thoughts. You will vibrate at a lower frequency with negative thoughts. You return to your natural state of vibration when you have no thoughts (as during meditation). The thoughts you believe and the words you speak have influence on you and everyone else. They have no power over you unless you focus on them and believe them. What are your thoughts right now? The best thing you can do in life is be very aware of your thoughts.

When you were a child, your parents molded your thought process by putting their thoughts and words in your head. You trusted and believed what they said to be true because they were your parents. What type of person are you? Are you typically happy and carefree? If your parents were easy-going and open-minded, then you are probably laid back and can easily form your own ideas and beliefs. Or are you doubtful and fearful? Perhaps your parents were pessimists. Perhaps you fit into all these categories. You are where you are in life primarily because of your thoughts. It could be a good place, or you might want to make some positive changes in your life.

Are you tormented by some of your thoughts? Should you believe all your thoughts? Do you know for sure what you are thinking is actually true? Our minds are very powerful and can conjure up a great story if we let them. Our minds can even provide a justification for the story. Now there may be some truth to the story, but our minds seem to magnify it. Our thoughts can sometimes fool us. We usually do not question our own thoughts, but we are quick to question other people's thoughts, especially when they differ from ours.

At one point in my life, I seriously believed all my thoughts because they were part of me. My mind came to a screeching halt the moment I realized I was not my thoughts. I can actually work with my thoughts, as long as I am aware of them, and weed out the ones that can cause problems. Although thoughts are a part of the human mind's function, our thoughts can play tricks on us. We have thoughts that deprive us of peace and happiness, and these are the ones we need to ignore. We should not believe all of our thoughts. We need to learn to accept and believe only the positive ones.

Observing your thoughts is a step in the right direction. Let them come and go in your head, and do not become attached to them unless they are good thoughts that you know are true. The way to accomplish this is by being alert. It is extremely important to be aware of what you are thinking at all times. You have to train yourself to do this so you can choose which ones to believe. You have thoughts you purposely think to clarify something, and then you have random ones that come into your head relating to any given moment. The random thoughts are the ones to question. Ask yourself: do I know for certain that this thought is true, and did this thought come into my mind unintentionally, or did I deliberately think it? Learn to discard the meaningless or negative ones that can disrupt your thought process. Sooner or later you will come to find out which ones to believe and which ones to ignore.

Every thought you believe creates some type of action. Your thoughts cannot hurt you unless you *think* they can. You can allow your thoughts to control you by believing every one you have. This is when you become a prisoner of your own mind. A new thought can quickly turn things around for you. When you have positive thoughts and a positive attitude, you will naturally attract more positive energy. You will attract positive people and situations to you. Remember, like attracts like. The same goes for negative thoughts. When you transmit negative energy, you will get negative results.

I have a very active mind (as most of us do). As much as I have learned about the thought process and being positive, to this day, a negative thought sometimes slips into my head. I choose to ignore it and stay focused so that it does not affect my emotions. I immediately replace it with as many positive thoughts that come to mind.

Your thoughts trigger your feelings, emotions, and behavior. Your emotions are your body's reactions to your mind and thoughts. You can actually think yourself into sadness or happiness. Do me a favor. The next time you are feeling down, unhappy, or depressed, ask yourself the following questions:

- Why am I feeling this way?
- What exactly is making me feel this way?
- Who is causing these emotions?
- When did I start experiencing these emotions?
- Are my thoughts making me upset?
- Are those thoughts really true?
- How do I know for sure that they are true?
- If I did not have those thoughts, would I be in a better mood?

By understanding your thoughts, you can change your mood. When you deal with your thoughts in a positive manner, you can control your emotions and behavior. So if you want to be happy, focus on the positive, constructive thoughts. You will gain much strength and confidence with positive thinking. When you concentrate on the positive thoughts, you will have more of them. Energy flows where attention goes. Believe and trust only the pure, caring, happy thoughts that come straight from the heart. You naturally know which ones they are.

We were all created equal and with good in us. Our thoughts, beliefs, and appearances are what make us different. The most important thing for us to remember is that our thoughts are not who we truly are. Our essence, inner being, inner voice, the power within, or whatever we want to label it, is who we really are.

So, if you want to change your life for the better, start being aware of your thoughts. Once you learn to judge your thoughts, you will make intelligent decisions, and your life will improve significantly. Master this process and you can master anything!

Negative Thoughts

Are you a negative person and are critical and complaining all the time? Negativity comes from fear, so ask yourself: what you are afraid of? Are you constantly fighting a battle with yourself? Our minds can be like a battleground. We cannot run away from ourselves, but we can make peace with our minds in order to achieve peace in life. Negative thoughts lower our vibrational frequency and cause suffering. They can be self-destructive and disconnect us from who we are. When we fight them, we are giving them power or significance. The harder we try to push them away, the longer they will stay. Resistance is persistence. Negative thoughts will interfere with our happiness. They can be toxic to the mind, body, and soul. When we have a negative attitude, we will attract more negative energy, and inner torment will surely affect our physical parts. The important message to understand here is the negative voices in your head cannot hurt you as long as you *pay no attention to them and disregard them.*

A negative thought is any thought of doubt, fear, worry, failure, criticism, envy, lack, distrust, spite, limitation, etc. regarding yourself or anyone else or anything. Our minds may be conditioned from the past with negative thinking. However, we can overcome this bad habit by changing the way we process our thoughts. Once you become aware of your thoughts, you can change your life. When negative thoughts come into your head, do not get upset with yourself for thinking them. They can be disturbing, but the most important thing for you to understand is that they are coming from somewhere other than your "real" self. Negative thoughts can draw you in totally when you give them attention. Ignore them and let them go. You will soon discover that they have less staying power than you realize. Place your awareness on all the positive ones.

When you say nice things to people, but in your mind you are thinking mean and hateful thoughts, sooner or later, your thoughts will turn into words, and words will evolve into action. You have to learn how to deal with the negative thoughts. The best way to do this is to dismiss them as soon as they come into your head. When you ignore the negative thoughts and place your focus on the good ones, the negative thoughts will weaken. Eventually they will go away, and you will have fewer negative thoughts. Acknowledge all positive aspects of yourself, the other person, place, thing, or situation. Stay on your toes and be ready to fill your mind with positive thoughts.

At first, it can be difficult to ignore the negative thoughts, but if you use the following method, it will get easier. When you recognize a negative thought, for example, *I hate her*, immediately turn it around and replace it with a positive thought which will counteract the original one. Purposely say to yourself, "I love her" or "she is a beautiful person." Then quickly think of another positive thought and keep feeding it with positive thoughts. Thoughts feed off other thoughts. As you continue to do this, the positive thoughts will overpower the negative ones.

Negative thoughts can be distracting, but you can rise above them. If you are having recurring negative thoughts about yourself and life, I encourage you to change your mindset. There is absolutely no reason for you to put yourself down. Destructive self-criticism can cause anxiety and lead to depression. Quit being so hard on yourself, and instead, focus on all of your positive accomplishments. You need to be telling yourself that you are someone *great*, because you truly are! An excellent way to overcome negative self-talk is to repeat positive affirmations.

Words are expressed through your thoughts and have power and energy just like your thoughts. Affirmations are when you are consciously declaring something to be true. Positive affirmations can be effective in building your confidence and self-esteem. First, you have to get rid of all the unhealthy beliefs that are deeply rooted in your subconscious mind. Healing codes have helped me to acknowledge my fears and insecurities from the past. I am open and receptive to new ideas and new ways to improve my life. You can visit their website for more information: http://www.healingcodescoaching.com.

Repeating positive affirmations may sound false to you, especially if you always doubt yourself. You are speaking the truth, because you already are what you are declaring. You may "think" that saying these words over and over will not help. I have done this, and I can honestly say this method really does work. I repeat them daily either silently or aloud while driving my car, lying in bed, or doing whatever. When you repeat them with confidence and determination, you will surely experience positive change in your life. Retrain your mind to believe all positive things about yourself. Tell yourself that you are courageous, strong, perfect, and beautiful in every way. Do not allow anyone else to tell you otherwise (especially you). Trust in the power of affirmations. Here is a powerful message for you to remember: you are what you think, feel, say, and believe you are! Author Mr. Bruce MacLelland's prosperity theology book, *Prosperity Through Thought Force* summarized the theory of thought vibration as, *"You are what you think, not what you think you are."*[12]

If are still bothered by negative thoughts, you can always turn to God for strength and guidance. Have faith in God and all things will always work out. Miracles are known to happen. Listen to your heart and your built-in guidance system. You truly are a wonderful person.

Ego

Do you know what the *ego* is? The ego is a functional part of the mind. Here is the definition from Dictionary.com: *"the 'I' or self of any person; a person as thinking, feeling, and willing, and distinguishing itself from the selves of others and from objects of its thought,"*[13] or in more simple terms, *"one's image of oneself."*

People may have different interpretations of the ego. Some think that the ego gives us that *drive* to do more and get more, but when it becomes overpowering and takes over our sense of identity, the ego can be destructive. You may ask, "If God created us with love and perfection, what is the purpose of the ego if it can be destructive?" All parts/states of the human structure, including physical, mental, social, spiritual, etc. are beneficial for experiencing life. When we become off-balance with any particular function, it can hinder our growth and well-being. We must do our best to keep our lives balanced with our thoughts and emotions under control.

God wants us to live good lives with great abundance. We have so many fine qualities that make us different from each other. God wants us to attain our goals and reach our destiny but not to the point of doing harm to ourselves or others.

---

12   "Law of attraction," rationalwiki.org, last modified August 1, 2014, http://rationalwiki.org/wiki/Law_of_attraction

13   Dictionary.com, s.v. "ego," accessed June 12, 2014, http://dictionary.reference.com/browse/ego?s=t&path=/

Certain people have egos that are easily recognizable on the surface. They are so into themselves and lack compassion and consideration for other people. They are arrogant and think they know it all. They will take credit for other people's work to gain recognition. They will step on other people's toes and do whatever it takes to get what they want. They are always searching for more by using people. The ego is controlling their lives. They are highly insensitive to other people's feelings, but little do they know, they are only hurting themselves. When they behave like this they may accomplish their goals in life, but they will lack peace within. When the ego is out of control, it can cause people to become narcissistic and loving themselves to the extent of vanity. I expand on the meaning of narcissism in Chapter 4: Living with Your Emotions. We must be very careful when we start accusing and blaming other people for our problems, when we should be examining ourselves to figure out how we can change our own behavior.

Egos can also be very subtle, and that is when they can be real problems. An example of this is when people look for appreciation when they do something good. It is the ego wanting attention. We are naturally humble and want to do good deeds out of the goodness of our hearts. But when we do it mainly for praise and glory, it is our egos demanding the spotlight.

Here are more warning signs of an inflated ego. It survives and breeds on misery. The ego is always searching for drama and needs to be right all the time. The ego does not like to be in the present moment. It likes to be in the past or the future so that it is in constant control. The ego is always bringing up old pain from the past and concern and worry about the future, thus causing pain and suffering. It likes competition and usually compares oneself to other people. The ego creates an image of oneself, and it could be good or bad.

There are three types of self-image: how you see yourself, how others see you, and how you perceive others see you. Your ego can create illusions that you are superior to others or the opposite that you are inadequate and not good enough. The ego creates false self-images from childhood experiences or past mind conditioning. You become identified with your thoughts and the way you perceive things. Pay attention to your thoughts so you know not to identify yourself with the ones that could cause problems. You must let go of those thoughts. The ego will eventually lose its power when it does not get the attention it needs.

When there are obstacles in life, the ego regards them as the enemy. However, these obstacles give us strength and the opportunity to grow. When you have faith in God and in yourself, you will overcome these difficulties, and there will be better days ahead. What we all need to do is be aware of our egos and keep them in check. We are great human beings created by God with much love. When there is love, compassion, and gratitude, the ego is not active. Let your heart and intuition guide you to achieve your desires. You will still succeed in life, and you will have peace and happiness within.

Law of Attraction

Do you know we can all have better lives, hang out with awesome people, and have some really cool things? The law of attraction, also known as the universal law, energy of attraction, power of thought, life energy force, vibrational frequency, law of awareness, or whatever you choose to call it is a simple way to manifest our desires. When I first heard about the law of attraction on the *Oprah Winfrey Show*, I was completely intrigued by it.

The following is a brief explanation of how this theory works: the law of attraction is a process that brings people, things, and events into our lives based on our thoughts and intentions. Everything in the universe (including human beings) is made up of energy and vibration. The universe works to make things happen and give you what you want (and possibly not want) by way of this powerful energy force.

The law of attraction is when "like attracts like," which means positive thoughts will bring you positive results, or it could be the opposite. Negative thoughts can produce negative results. Feelings of depression and unhappiness will attract negative energy and affect your body physically. *You* can actually control the type of energy you are attracting. Once you consciously or unconsciously think a thought, a specific vibration or signal is sent out to the universe. When you keep thinking the same thought, the vibration will get stronger. Have you ever thought about someone, and then all of a sudden that person appeared, or you got a phone call or e-mail from him or her? It is no coincidence. You actually attracted them to you by the theories and laws of the universe. It is the law of attraction in action. What you are seeking is seeking you.

Have you ever heard the saying, "Be careful what you wish for, because you just might get it all?" When you ask for something, do it with intention and awareness so that you get exactly what you want. You have to be careful when asking for something you want now but may regret later.

Here is how it works. Think about what you want. Once you define your desire, let it be known to God. You must be perfectly clear about what you want. Picture it in your mind to get a clear vision. You cannot have any doubt or contradicting thoughts about it, or it will take longer for you to manifest it. Manifest means to bring about, make evident, or make certain by showing or displaying. Imagine yourself in the picture and playing out the part. It does not matter how big it is or how much it costs. Visualization helps solidify the process. Take action, start preparing for it, and act like you already have it. To speed up the process, you can write it down, draw it, cut out a picture of it, and hang it up where you can constantly see it. If it is a material item, move things around and figure out where you are going to place it. Get enthused and excited about it and feel the emotions. By doing all of this, you will get it much quicker. Do not worry about how or when it is going to happen; have faith it will happen. Believe and you will receive. Be aware of your thoughts.

Positive thoughts will bring you coordinating results. Do not obsess over it, or you will drive it away. Forget about it, trust in God, and watch what happens. Before you know it, voilà ... there it is. God created a very friendly universe, and you can have what you desire. So dream *big*!

Here is something important to remember about the law of attraction and the universe. Your thoughts and words play a huge role in attracting people, things, or situations to you. In order to control what you attract, you must be conscious of what your intentions are and what you are thinking. Your thoughts will turn into words, words into actions, and ultimately you will create experiences. Become aware of your thoughts so that you can be selective about the words you speak. When we are not conscious, we tend to automatically use words that are sometimes to our disadvantage and end up attracting things we do not want.

Sometimes the universe will have a different translation of your words. The universe does not recognize negative words like *don't*, *not*, or *no*, so those types of words are canceled out. The next time you say something like, "I do not want to be late," the universe will pick up the word *late*, and therefore, you will be late. Do not focus your attention on what you do *not* want (unless you really want it to happen). Fix your thoughts on what you *do* want, and be very clear about it. Say something positive, such as, "I am going to be on time," and when you repeat it and believe it, you will be on time. Here is another example. If your arm has been bothering you, and the pain has finally subsided, do not say, "My arm doesn't hurt anymore." The universe will focus directly on the word *hurt*, and guess what will happen ... the pain will come back. Instead say something positive like, "My arm feels great!"

Have you ever heard the expression, "Never say never?" It means that even if you say, "I never want to move back home again," you may end up moving back home. Why? Because the universe cancels out *never* and picks up on *I want to move back home again*. Whatever you do not want to happen may happen anyway because of the words stated. The universe will give you exactly what you ask for, so be mindful of what you are thinking and saying. We should stay away from words like *battling, combatting, fighting, crime, warriors, war*, etc., because that is exactly what we are going to get. We need to use positive, inspiring words if we want more peace, love, joy, and harmony in this world.

Here is another example to help you understand. When you say you are *trying* to do this or that, you will get exactly what you are transmitting to the universe. You will continue trying, and you will not get anywhere. You have to change your words. This time, leave out the word trying and use these two very powerful words *I am*. For instance, change this sentence from, "I am trying to quit smoking" to "I am quitting smoking." (Review the section about negative thoughts again.) Better yet, take action and do it!

The best part about this beautiful world in which we live is there is an abundance of everything. There is plenty to go around for everyone, no matter what it is that you want! There is no need to be greedy, and you do not have to sacrifice anything to get it. Lose the thoughts of lack or scarcity. If you want to give up something, that is a different scenario. When you feel like you *have to* make a sacrifice, you will not feel good about it. Willingly do things that make you feel good and high-spirited!

We live in a material world, and God wants us to enjoy the nice things in life. Mankind has created these things with their God-given talent. However, you must always remember to be grateful and appreciate what you have, because it all can be taken away in a blink of an eye. I would like to share with you this quote, which was written by spiritual leader Dr. Michael Beckwith: *"Nothing new can come into your life, unless you open yourself up to being grateful."*[14]

---

[14] "It's All About Gratitude," TheSecretProgram.com, accessed August 14, 2014, http://thesecretprogram.com

CHAPTER 4

Living with Your Emotions

Anger Within

Do you get frustrated with yourself when you cannot do something right? Do you beat yourself up or feel you are not good enough? Do you know what you are doing to yourself when you get angry? Internal anger and conflict causes health problems. When you think unkind thoughts, you are only hurting yourself inside and out. These thoughts and feelings are obstacles that prevent you from being happy. You lose the courage and ambition to become who God made you to be. Be aware of your negative thoughts and emotions so that you can change the way you feel about yourself. There is no need to be an angry person. Have a change of heart. You were created with the same power within you as everyone else, and with this divine power, you can achieve your desires.

The first step in dealing with anger is to recognize that you are angry. Once you know this, you have to figure out what is making you mad and that it is really not worth getting that upset over. Are you trying to control someone or a situation? Although things might not be going your way, you have to become detached from the outcome. Be positive that everything will work out.

When you are angry with yourself, do you find that you quickly get annoyed with other people? Keep in mind that whatever energy you put out to the universe is what you are going to get in return. When you are angry and upset, you tend to say things you do not really mean. When you act like this, you are only hurting yourself. Would you want this kind of treatment? You are going to get it right back at you whether you want it or not.

People who are hurting may also be hurting other people—but not intentionally. They are not even aware of it because they are so caught up with their own emotions. Have you ever heard the quote: *"He who angers you conquers you"*[15] written by Australian celebrity, Ms. Elizabeth Kenny? Getting angry resolves nothing. When you feel like you are about to lose it with someone who is already upset, do your best to stay composed. Some people have anger within them that they have to release. People that lash out at other people are the ones who are the weakest and suffering the most. Accept these people for who they are during this time and understand why they are behaving this way. You want to avoid falling into the same pattern of behavior. Stay calm and resolve the issue in a reasonable manner. You can walk away to prevent an argument from escalating. Always keep your emotions under control.

Another way of understanding the quote, *"He who angers you conquers you,"* is when there is a confrontation between two people and one person is sensible enough not to react to the other person's bad behavior. The other person gets angry, because no reaction is involved and his or her plan actually backfires. In reality, you have conquered that person. Be the better person by not reacting to negative behavior and settling things rationally.

Anger Toward God

Do you ever get mad at God, especially when things are going great and then BAM something bad happens (at least we think so at the time). Sometimes our plan does not work out, and the situation

---

[15] BrainyQuote.com, accessed August 15, 2014, http://www.brainyquote.com/quotes/quotes/e/elizabethk100902.html

seems unfair. It has happened to all of us. Typically, our minds magnify the situation, and we just want to cry! We immediately ask why. Why did this happen, what am I doing wrong, why are things not working out, etc. It is particularly hard on parents when it happens to their children. Some parents would rather take the fall than see their children suffer. But this would only prevent them from becoming independent. God wants every one of us to be strong and responsible but yet loving and compassionate. How would we learn to be good if we do not experience bad? How would we know about light if we did not have dark? We have to learn to accept things as they are whether it is something major or minor, because it is all part of life's lessons. Even when we experience failure, we have to keep the faith and be grateful no matter what circumstances arise. If you think you have it so bad, take a look around, then you will not complain about your problems.

There are many situations in this world we cannot control. When something negative happens to you, consider it a challenge. See it as something separate from you and is only temporary. When you view it this way, you will be able to control your reaction and address the situation with a clear mind. You can be certain that once you get through it, you will be a lot wiser.

I am sure you have heard these words before: *"everything happens for a reason."* (I am not referring to karma here.) I want those words to really sink in. Remember them and repeat them to yourself when negative situations arise. When people talk about how their lives are not going so well, I want you to understand what you are saying when you automatically reply, "Everything happens for a reason." We can easily say this, but when it actually happens to us, do we keep our cool and remember those words? This is when the true test of faith comes in. Even though there is no logical explanation at the time, we should not get angry and blame God or anybody for the situation. Perhaps God interfered with what was about to happen in order to spare someone's life. So either way, we have to accept whatever is happening and know there is a reason behind everything. Do not try to figure things out. Let it go, and let it be. It is what it is. Of course, when a challenge arises, we have to address it appropriately. The good news is these trials and tribulations could force us into consciousness.

We learn and progress from these types of experiences, and the lessons we learn will last a lifetime. We gain more strength and courage to overcome obstacles with the greatest force helping us. We become empowered to achieve our goals and to fulfill our assignments in life. Use these experiences as stepping stones. It is funny because we always seem to remember the difficult times in our lives. Besides, at that time it may have seemed unfortunate, but when you think back, perhaps it was not so bad after all. There is a time for everything, and it happens in perfect order.

You can think of it this way: there is always love coming from God, and something wonderful is in store for you. You can say to yourself, "Everything happens for *me*." God is working behind the scenes to give you what you want, but things must occur in natural order. Go with the flow; do not try to paddle upstream, because it will only be a struggle. When you swim against the flow of water, it becomes more difficult and exhausting, especially when the current gets stronger. Changing your stroke is not the answer either, but if you change your direction, swim with the current and work with it; everything will flow accordingly. Be like a swan in the water and just go where the current takes you. Let God guide you, because God is in control and always on your side.

Remember that karma thing. At one time, maybe you did not make a mistake, but you made the wrong choice. You were not mindful of what you were doing when you made the choice. It is all right because you can shift your frequency into a different level at any given moment despite what happened in the past. Everything is as it should be, and you will get back the same energy as you transmit. That is why it is very important to be aware of your thoughts and actions at all times.

You may ask about losing a loved one or a baby or young child. Why does this happen? Yes, losing loved ones is tragic, but it is their time to physically leave this world. People come into our lives and go for a reason, but we must keep pressing forward with our own lives. Sooner or later, we will all be doing the same. Be grateful to have known them, even if it was for a short time, and for the fond memories and the time you spent with them. We cannot question why it happened because we cannot see the big picture. Trust that it was for a good cause.

When you are having a rough day and things are not going your way, it is time to start over again and wipe the slate clean. You do not have to wait until the next day to change things. Start the moment you realize it. Tell yourself that everything is going to be all right, and things are going to improve from this point forward. A good way to overcome adversity is to operate in an opposing manner. Where there is hatred, promote love; where there is anger, promote peace; where there is depression, promote encouragement; etc. I recommend beginning each day with thanking God in advance for all your blessings and being with you and providing you guidance throughout the day. When things get tough, keep this in mind: setbacks are actually a step forward to where you should be. Always maintain your enthusiasm, courage, and confidence.

Fear

Fear is when you worry about something bad happening that has not even happened yet. What are your fears? When you were a child, were you afraid of the dark or being alone? Perhaps you still are. Most people generally have fear of the unknown. One of our biggest fears is the fear of death and how we are going to die. We fear death because we do not know what to expect. Is it horrible or peaceful? There are people who claim they have had near-death experiences. There are some people who said they have actually experienced the death transition into the non-physical world, and it was very peaceful. We have all experienced fear at one point or another in our lives. Even the strongest, bravest people get scared. There is no need to try to hide your fears or be ashamed of them. In fact, knowing and acknowledging your fears may be more comforting.

Fear is everything negative that weakens the soul. When we lack faith and trust in God and in ourselves, we experience fear. Fear is the result of being separated or disconnected from the source of our creation. Once we reestablish that connection again, we will feel more safe, secure, and at peace. The solution to overcome fear is to stay connected with God.

To begin with, we were born with love and peace within, but eventually we learned fear. If we trace back to the source of our fears, we may discover that one of our parents had some of the same fears. If we can overcome our fears or be more conscious of them, there will be fewer chances that our children will be affected by them. They will grow up being more courageous and confident.

It is easy to say face your fears, but how do you do that? How do you get up enough courage to face your fears? Not being afraid to do something is not courage. Courage is doing it while being afraid. Usually, when you are about to go through a change in your life, you will experience some fear. Fear has a lot to do with your thoughts. Question your thoughts. Are they true, and how do you know for sure? Remember, negative thoughts will attract negative energy. However, when you consider this change as an exciting new adventure and opportunity to grow, you will move forward with a different perspective. Think of it as a challenge and get psyched about it. Turn the thought of fear around in your mind, and focus on this change as being a positive experience. You are safe, and everything will work out as it should.

Many of us have the fear of failure. Have you ever gotten upset with yourself after you worked long and hard on a project and it failed? You have to give yourself credit for trying. At least you can say you gave it your best shot. Are we afraid to fail because we are so concerned about what others will think? Guess what … they are going to fail too. Everyone fails at one point or another in life. We learn from our mistakes. Failure is good. I repeat: failure is good. Failure actually gives us strength and determination. It is God's way of telling us to try a new approach or there is something better in the works. Failure is success in disguise. When we experience failure, we can appreciate success. Continue to do your best and be your best.

One of our fears could be that we are afraid of the deep, dark thoughts and feelings we have inside us. We are not those thoughts. They are coming from somewhere else. And we are not powerless, because we have access to Godlike power within us to overcome those troubled thoughts. We should not fear this power either, but rather take advantage of it. This power will help us to improve and strengthen our cognitive abilities. Internationally acclaimed spiritual author Ms. Marianne Williamson says this about fear: *"Our deepest fear is not that we are inadequate. Our deepest fear is that we are powerful beyond measure. It is our light, not our darkness that most frightens us."*[16]

Horror movies or movies with violence and scary books can put ugly thoughts in our heads. Watching the news or reading the newspaper can put fear in us and cause us to worry about the future. Watch educational programs or read books that have value.

The next time you are faced with fear, put your faith and trust in God and yourself. You can talk to God like a friend at any time. Wherever you are, God is there for you and always will be. God is a part of you. Ask God to help you realize that you have the strength and courage to rise above your fears. I know your fears will slowly diminish, and the divine power within you will dominate. Look fear in the eyes. Fear will blink first.

Finally, if you have done all you can to overcome a specific fear, then stop, and focus on what gives you enjoyment and confidence.

---

[16] "Marianne Williamson > Quotes," Goodreads.com, accessed September 24, 2014, http://www.goodreads.com/author/quotes/17297. Marianne_Williamson

There are so many opportunities in this world. Why stress over something that continually gives you anxiety? Appreciate your talents and strengths and concentrate on your positive energy. Be brave, be bold, and be better.

Worry

Do you ever feel like you are carrying around a huge sack of worries that is dragging you down to the ground? I bet if you look inside that sack, it would be empty, because you have nothing to worry about. Worry takes the glory out of each precious moment. Worry causes uneasiness and inner turmoil. We imagine things happening that will probably never happen. If you have to be suspicious, be suspicious of your thoughts. Basically, there is nothing to fear but ourselves and what we are thinking. We can consciously control our lives and the situations we get ourselves into. When you stay positive and do the right things in life, you will experience a boundless and limitless life. You will live a more peaceful and satisfying life because there will be nothing to fear.

Fear and worry cause unnecessary anxiety and suffering. They are similar in that you are already thinking about the possible outcome of a situation. You are worried that something may not work out. You are having doubt. You are thinking about the future instead of being focused on the here and now. Pay attention to what is presently going on in your life instead of worrying about what could happen. Worrying is a waste of valuable time. What if everything works out perfectly and you did all that worrying for nothing?

Worrying will surely affect your health. Stress is a symptom caused from fear, worry, and other negative emotions. You may also experience lack of sleep, achiness, nervousness, anxiety, high blood pressure, etc. Stress is a leading cause of many health issues today. Stress suppresses the immune system and drains your energy. Do you stress easily over studying for tests, financial commitments, your job, taking care of children, etc.? These are normal things that we all have to do, and they can become overwhelming at times and easily cause stress. Balance your time so that you have an equal amount of quality time to spend on yourself.

My parents were my first teachers, and I learned so many good things from them, but I also learned some not-so-good things. My parents constantly worried about everything. When they worried about their children, I used to think it was a sign of love and compassion. Oh, they certainly were loving parents, but their worrying affected their family in a negative way. I soon developed this negative nature, and unfortunately, I have passed this condition on to my own daughters. My parents were overprotective, and it is not good to try to control every situation. Worrying is predicting the future. It does not help matters, and it could actually attract a negative situation.

Your mind can be so convincing, and if you give power and energy to your thoughts and think the same ones over and over again, you could bring those thoughts into action. I used to worry about things I had no control over. However, I *do* have control over my thoughts, words, and actions. I have faith that all will work out as it should. I am pleased to report that I am more optimistic about the future. Oh, there are times when the old conditioned mind patterns come back, but as long as I am *aware* of my thoughts, I can break the pattern. It is senseless to worry, because you are only wasting valuable time.

Do you worry about what people think of you? When you find yourself worrying about what people say about you, remember this: the less approval you seek, the more approval you will get. God is the one you should be impressing. Here is a good book title written by Ms. Terry Cole-Whittaker: *"What You Think of Me is None of My Business."*[17] Instead of worrying about what people think of you, believe in yourself. When you have negative thoughts about yourself,

---

[17]   Terry Cole-Whittaker, *"What You Think of Me is None of My Business"* First published 1979 by Oak Tree Publications, San Diego, CA

change them at once to confident thoughts. I used to constantly seek approval from other people, but I never seemed to get it. The harder I tried to gain their love, respect, and approval, the less of it I got. Now, the most important thing that matters to me is seeking God's approval and my own.

Guilt and Regret

Do you have a guilty conscience for something you said or did in the past that was wrong or hurtful? When you do something that is not right, especially when you know it is not right, you will not feel good about yourself. The guilt you are feeling is normal and for a purpose. Although these emotions may be trying to teach you a lesson to make better choices, it is also important for you to learn how to handle them. Do not identify with negative thoughts or feelings of regret and resentment. This will prolong the healing process. Dwelling on thoughts about the past will keep you stuck in a rut. When you forgive yourself in a healthy, positive way, and humble yourself, you will be able to move forward with life.

When you were younger, did you ever say or do something wrong, and your parents were very upset with you? Do you still regret it to this day? Growing up, you naturally wanted to please your parents, but there were times when you messed up. That is okay because you were learning to be independent and to follow your own path. Those experiences help you grow and become a mature adult. To this day, I continue to learn about life. Regret weighs heavily on your mind, so it is time to praise yourself for all the things you are doing so well.

Have you ever blamed yourself for something bad that happened that you could have possibly prevented if you had done something or told someone about it? When you are feeling guilty about a situation like this, it is an emotional response to something you should not feel guilty about. In certain situations, things are beyond our control, and if at the time of the incident you did not react, then you were not guided to. Your instinct was to not interfere with what was supposed to happen. Let it go and forgive yourself.

The next time you have guilt or regret about something you have done in the past, examine your thoughts. Ask yourself, "Am I really to blame, or is it just an unreasonable response to a situation?" On a more positive note, whatever you are feeling guilty about is over and done with. So why keep thinking about it? Do not be so hard on yourself. Tell yourself it is all right to make mistakes, and if it makes you feel any better, everyone makes them. You have already been forgiven by God, so you should forgive yourself. Today is a brand new day with a new beginning. Keep a positive attitude and move forward.

Happiness

Why are there are so many unhappy people in this world? Do you know that you can choose to be happy? If you are miserable, do not just sit there and whine about how unhappy you are and what is not working in your life. Do something about it and intentionally be happy. *"It is better to light a candle than to curse the darkness"* is a Chinese proverb that means it is better to do something about a problem than complain about it. When you choose to be happy, at that point in your life, you will see how quickly things will change for the better. I totally agree with what Ms. Oprah Winfrey says about finding happiness: *"The way to choose happiness is to follow what is right and real, the truth for you. You can never be happy living someone else's dream. Live your own. Then you will know the meaning of happiness for sure."*[18]

If I were given one wish for everyone in life, that wish would be for happiness. Do you know that in reality happiness leads you

---

[18] Oprah Winfrey, "Oprah Shares How to Choose Happiness," *The Oprah Magazine South Africa*, February 2014, http://www.oprahmag.co.za/live-your-best-life/self-development/oprah-shares-how-to-choose-happiness

to be more productive and successful? Happy people are generally healthier people, because they experience less stress in their lives. They do not require medication, drugs, or alcohol to cope with life.

Happiness is an internal state. There are many happy people in this world who do not have a whole lot of money or material things, but yet they are happy. Why? Because they accept themselves for who they are, they appreciate what they do have, and they make the best of life. Their happiness is not based upon external status.

Money can provide a certain fulfillment, but money cannot buy happiness. Below are four possible scenarios for happiness and money:

a. You can be unhappy and have no money.
b. You can be unhappy and have money.
c. You can be happy and have no money.
d. You can be happy and have money.

Which of the four scenarios above is the best approach for a balanced life? I would select letter "d" above because I want it all! If you start by being happy with yourself and life, you will have a much better chance of being financially stable. While we are on the subject of money, you may have heard people say this before: "Money does not grow on trees" or "Money is the root of all evil." No, no, no. Some of us need to reprogram our minds about money messages. God wants us all to be happy and prosperous and to enjoy nice things in life. Money does not create evil; however, I know for sure that your thoughts can. Negative thoughts could lead you to bad behavior. Fear, doubt, worry, and insecurity are the root causes of evil.

Happy people are usually successful. Many people think that if you are successful you will be happy, but that is not always the case. You can be a billionaire and still be unhappy. This is more like a state of satisfaction. Material objects will satisfy you temporarily, but eventually, you will get bored with them and want something else. The same principle applies to physical changes. You can be drop-dead gorgeous, but you are going to grow old. You can make all the changes you want to your hair, face, or body, but you will soon want to change something else. Change is good, and I encourage you to try new things, but you cannot depend on them for happiness. It is so exciting to buy a new car, change your hairstyle, go on a vacation, etc. You will be satisfied for a short while, but then the vicious cycle will continue. Chances are you will go back to being the same discontented person. You are seeking happiness through things, but the things cannot give you permanent happiness. The condition of our inner beings is far more important than owning a material thing. Working on the inside to become better, content, and emotionally stable is priority. You can have the best of both worlds, but concentrate on being happy with yourself first. It seems when you achieve happiness and peace within, quality will matter more than quantity.

Things will not give you real happiness and neither will people. You should not depend on anybody to make you happy—not your boyfriend, girlfriend, mom, dad, friend, relative, or anybody else. When you rely on other people for your happiness, you are setting yourself up for disappointment. You may experience happiness with someone temporarily, but the minute they say or do something you disagree with, you become annoyed with that person. They are not you. You know what you want and need to bring you happiness. If you are looking for someone to make you happy, look in the mirror. Once you are completely happy with yourself, you will be able to accept people for who they are, and you will have healthier relationships.

So how do we get this happiness? The happiness I am talking about comes from within. We create this happiness with a positive frame of mind, a happy heart, and a happy soul, under any circumstances—good or bad. We are normally happy when good things happen. But when we have true happiness within, we will not let negative situations affect this happiness. When we are happy, we

will attract more positive energy. We will attract other happy people, because they will enjoy being in our company.

First, choose to be happy and tell yourself, "I am very happy." Continually tell yourself this every day. When you are having a bad day, tell yourself that you are happy and everything is as it should be. Second, start focusing on yourself and figure out ways to make you happy and what you enjoy doing. Do things to make you happy and content with life. If you are constantly trying to please other people, you will be unhappy. *You have to make you happy.*

Moods are contagious and can rub off on other people if they allow it. Have you ever noticed that when somebody is in a bad mood, it sometimes can put you in a bad mood? Bad moods are contagious too. When someone is in a bad mood, and if you can *recognize* it at that time, do not let their mood affect your happiness. Be positive and say something to counteract that person's negative behavior. When you are in control of yourself, no matter what kind of mood people are in, you will stay in a good frame of mind. The key is to be *aware* of yourself and other people's moods.

Question your thoughts, because they play a critical role in your happiness. Be aware of what you are thinking, and know that your *true* self is not your thoughts. Your mind could be so conditioned from the past, so when your thoughts are not good, you can either ignore them or change them. Once you do this, it will be like the domino effect. Everything else will change accordingly, and things will fall into place.

Since you will not achieve happiness within yourself through acquiring material things or looking beautiful, you may ask yourself, "Well, then what does bring me happiness?" If you think a loving thought, speak a kind word, or do a good deed every day, not only will you feel contentment, but you will also make someone else's day brighter.

The following is a list of some other examples of things you can do that will make you feel good inside. As always, do them without *expecting* something in return (you will usually get it back anyway).

Remember, when you feel good about yourself, you will be happy and feel good about life. Here are some simple things to do that will bring you joy:

- Cuddling a newborn baby
- Playing with a young child and acting like a child yourself
- Playing with a puppy, kitten, or any pet
- Lying in the grass on a clear summer night and looking up at the stars
- Giving something to someone, even if it is small, regifted, or handmade
- Helping someone with anything
- Giving someone a compliment and meaning it
- Taking a walk anywhere outside and breathing fresh air
- Hugging or kissing someone
- Smiling at everyone (you just might change someone's attitude)
- Visiting someone in the hospital, nursing home, or jail
- Opening the door or holding the door for someone
- Realizing the beauty of a flower, plant, bird, or animal
- Going outside when it is snowing or raining and enjoying the quietness and wonder of it all coming down from the sky
- Saying "Thank you very much" to whomever for whatever and being grateful
- Listening to someone as he or she is going through a difficult time
- Watching the sunrise or the sunset
- Sending a greeting card, e-mail, or letter to someone to let that person know you were thinking about him or her and that you care
- Calling someone just to say hello and to see how they are doing
- Creating or designing something yourself (painting, drawing, photographing, woodworking, etc.)

- Writing what you are grateful for in a journal
- Appreciating everything life has to offer

When you look at the list, you will notice each item begins with a verb, which means some kind of action or effort is required on your part. You will always feel good when you accomplish something. Do not just sit there being idle and bored and complaining all the time with nothing to do. Instead of focusing on an activity, you will start focusing on your thoughts, and that is when you can get yourself into trouble. Most of the items on the list do not cost much, if anything, so there are no excuses. You will notice that watching television is not listed. There are some great educational programs on television, but then there are some shows that are downright ridiculous. Be selective about which programs or movies you watch and which ones you avoid.

Happiness is a choice and takes strength of mind, so it is totally up to you. You can choose to make some positive changes in your life and be happy, or you can choose to stay the same. When you focus on the positive things, you will attract positive people and events to you. The way you choose to live your life will determine your happiness, so be happy *now*! Choose to be happy, and amazing things will happen!

Love

Every single person wants to hear these three words: I love you. Love is the highest, most powerful form of positive energy in the universe. God created everyone and everything with love; hence, everyone has love within them. Love is the greatest gift we have. Love is pure, complete, and absolute acceptance. Love is happiness, joy, and everything positive. Love illuminates everything. Love is more than just romance or personal attachment. Love is also having compassion and affection toward oneself and all other beings. Dr. Martin Luther King Jr. summed it up perfectly:

Hatred paralyzes life; love releases it.
Hatred confuses life; love harmonizes it.
Hatred darkens life; love illumines it.[19]

Do you love yourself? God wants you to love, honor, appreciate, and respect yourself for all that you are. Love every part of yourself inside and out, including what you may call flaws or imperfections. This is difficult for many people to do, but loving yourself is the most essential part of living your best life.

Love yourself the right way without being self-centered, conceited, or narcissistic. Here is the definition of the word *conceited* from Dictionary.com: *"having an excessively favorable opinion of one's abilities, appearance, etc. Synonyms: vain, proud, egotistical, self-important, self-satisfied."*[20]

The definition of the word narcissism *from Dictionary.com is* "inordinate fascination with oneself; excessive self-love; vanity. Synonyms: self-centeredness, smugness, egocentrism."[21] There is a fine line between loving yourself and being narcissistic. Being narcissistic is when the ego is out of control and distracts you from your spiritual self. Love yourself in such a way that is not arrogant or narcissistic, a way in which you have pure, kind, and loving thoughts about yourself. Love yourself the way God loves us. We all came from the same source and were created in the image and likeness of God. We may think differently and have different appearances, but we have the same spiritual essence. Take a selfie (a picture of yourself typically taken with a cell phone camera and you holding the phone) and love your selfie!

---

[19] Values.com, accessed August 19, 2014, http://www.values.com/inspirational-quotes/3687-Hatred-Paralyzes-Life-Love-

[20] Dictionary.com, s.v. "conceited," accessed August 18, 2014, http://dictionary.reference.com/browse/conceited?s=t

[21] Dictionary.com, s.v. "narcissism," accessed August 18, 2014, http://dictionary.reference.com/browse/narcissism?s=t

You must love your physical qualities and characteristics, including the ones you dislike. A feature that is regarded as unfavorable is sometimes called a flaw. These features are actually what make you different from everyone else. They are not ugly or bad, but society views them as things to fix. This is why we feel inferior around others and become insecure and self-conscious of our appearances. We should embrace our imperfections, because we were made by God as unique individuals. The physical part of you is insignificant compared to the true essence of who you are. What you are inside your body is flawless!

Do you ever talk to yourself? When you have an inner dialogue, be sure to ignore the negative words. Criticizing yourself and comparing yourself with other people will harm you. You are one of a kind, and God wants you to love yourself as you are. Love every part, inside and out. Compliment yourself and be kind to yourself just as you would with someone else. Look in the mirror every day and say, "Thank you for creating me so perfect!" When you love and appreciate everything about yourself, you will experience positive changes in your life and in your physical appearance. You will reflect that special glow of happiness. Love nourishes health. Not only will you look happy, but you will feel healthy. God wants you to take care of yourself just like you would nurture a child.

You were created whole and perfect and in alignment with God. When you believe this, you will believe in yourself. When you appreciate yourself, you will attract all good things and achieve your desires. When you are feeling separate and resisting your authentic self, you will experience fear. You will feel bad about yourself; thus, you will attract negativity in your life. May I make a small suggestion? Get some sticky notes and write down all the things you love about yourself. You will realize just how wonderful you are! Put the sticky notes up where you can see them every day to remind yourself of this. When you want to change for the better, you have to change the way you think and feel about yourself!

You were created with love, and you are a wonderful human being. You are a beautiful person with a loving heart. Do not let your negative thoughts or anyone discourage you. You have to love yourself before you can love anyone else. When you love and respect yourself, you will be able to love other people. You will love them for who they are, what they are, and how they behave, with complete and total acceptance. You might say you love someone because of his or her characteristics, good looks, or his or her charming personality, but that is not love. You *like* someone conditionally. God loves us with total and complete love, and so it is easy for us to love our children this way. We must love our neighbors by loving the oneness within them, which is the same oneness in you. This does not mean loving them for the way they maintain their homes or the way they dress, etc. We must love everyone, even our so-called enemies.

Do you ever wonder why we are supposed to love our enemies? We should love without conditions, and forgive people for their mistakes. Believe it or not, people filled with anger and hatred also have love within them. Remember that God created all of us with pure love. There is goodness in everyone, and where there is goodness, there is God. They, too, may be struggling to uncover the truth about life. We should still show love and respect toward them. They are human beings too, although at times they may not behave like one. They have already suffered enough with their negative thoughts and poor choices, so look for their goodness and love them anyway.

Here is the most beautiful passage on love that I have read and would like to share with you. It is based on a passage from 1 Corinthians Chapter 13, a beloved chapter in the Bible that covers the subject of love. Many young couples have this scripture recited at their weddings. It is good to remember these words when the road gets rocky in a marriage or relationship. Please read it with total awareness.

Love

Love is patient;
love is kind
and envies no one.
Love is never boastful,
nor conceited, nor rude;
never selfish,
not quick to take offense.

Love keeps no score
of wrongs; does not gloat
over another's sins,
but delights in the truth.
There is nothing
love cannot face;
there is no limit
to its faith, its hope,
and its endurance.

In a word,
there are three things
that last forever:
faith, hope and love;
but the greatest
of them all
is love.[22]

We were created by love, we are love, we love to be *in* love, we love to love, and we love to be loved. When there is love, no matter what the circumstances may be, there is light. Love is the guiding positive energy force for life. Do me a favor. Every day tell someone you love them (including yourself). One time I sent a bunch of text

---

[22] Urban Dictionary.com, last modified January 30, 2004, http://www. urbandictionary.com/define.php?term=love&defid=480188

messages to some friends and relatives just to tell them that I love them. I got a lot of "love you's" back too.

A human body can still function without certain organs or body parts, but it cannot live without a heart. Let your love flow freely today.

CHAPTER 5

Controlling Your Behavior

Karma

Do you believe in karma? Karma is also called the law of cause and effect. It is similar to the law of attraction, but it is based on your actions. Have you ever heard the saying, "What goes around comes around?" Whatever type of energy you are transmitting to the world, you will attract that same type of energy. This is a fact. This philosophy is so simple and logical. There is good and bad karma. So you can create a good life as long as you are aware of your actions.

This is how karma works. Your behavior toward others is exactly what you will get in return. It may be now or it may be later, but the cycle absolutely works. You could be totally blindsided one day due to past events. As expected, if you are rude to someone, you will be treated in the same disrespectful manner. If you are an honest, trustworthy person, you will be able to trust other people, and they will trust you. When you give love, you will get love. When you treat people with kindness and courtesy, people will be kind and polite toward you. People will give you more attention when you are attentive to them. Giving is receiving. You reap what you sow.

Your thoughts are aligned with your actions, so your behavior is a result of what you are thinking. Good behavior comes from positive thoughts and bad behavior is caused by negative thinking.

Whatever your actions are, you will get that same force of energy right back at you. When you intentionally hurt someone, you are also hurting yourself. How many times does it have to happen before you realize this is the real deal? Negative thoughts, words, and actions will come back to sting you, and it is going to hurt. The following quote is a good way of explaining it: *"Karma has no menu; you get served what you deserve!"*[23]

Do you want to live life with a clear conscience? Do you want to quit worrying whether or not something bad is going to happen? You have to be the way you want to be treated. The good thing is, if you have been experiencing bad karma lately, you can change it by modifying your behavior and being mindful of your thoughts and actions. Change can be challenging, but you can do it. Pray to God for help and guidance. Base your choices on love and compassion instead of fear and doubt. This will bring more positive karma into your life. Remember, when there is an action, there is a reaction.

Reaction

How do you react when someone does something mean or hurtful to you? How do you respond when someone blames you for something you did not do? Your immediate reaction sometimes is to attack back, defend yourself, or get even, but that is not the correct way to resolve issues. You will only be acting the same way as the other person, because it is your ego working against you. The confrontation will probably escalate and result in a disagreement or argument. Emotions can quickly flare up. Pretty soon you will both end up saying or doing things you may regret later.

I am sure you have witnessed people get completely out of control, screaming and yelling at each other. Their faces get blood red and veins pop out on their foreheads. Obviously, they are unaware of their behavior. Imagine what it is doing to the insides of their

---

[23]   Author unknown

bodies. Regrettably, a lot of us have been there and done that, maybe not to that extreme, but enough to cause a lot of distress. Practice controlling your emotions at all times, especially when you feel you are getting angry. This next part you might not agree with, but sometimes you just have to suck it up, take the blame for whatever, and move on. You have to demonstrate to the other person that you are the more mature, sensible one. Would you rather be right or have peace within?

Instead of overreacting, keep things in perspective. Always practice self-control and stay composed. Do the right thing by exhibiting acceptable behavior (see the section about balance). Before reacting, take a few deep breaths, and settle yourself down. Be strong and stand up for what you know is right, but in a decent way. You are not a doormat either, so do not let people take advantage of you. People will treat you the way you let them. You should not tolerate bad behavior. In any case, keep balance in your life.

No matter what the situation is, nothing is worth getting upset over. Be the peacemaker. Do not let anyone get the best of you. You must forgive that person immediately. One day, that person will learn a valuable lesson (karma). We need to put matters into God's hands instead of trying to handle things ourselves. Sometimes we have no choice in certain situations, but we can choose how we react to them. You can control the situation by controlling your emotions. It is better to respond appropriately than to react irrationally. God will take care of the people who behave inappropriately. God will also take care of the people who do what is right.

You will have setbacks in life. It is okay and actually healthy to let your emotions flow freely, especially when you are feeling sad or depressed. It is not good to keep them all pent up inside. There is a time and a place to release these emotions. The first thing I would do is connect with God. God helps those to learn to help themselves. You have to want to help yourself. In your own private space, let go of everything that is bothering you. If you want to cry, have a good cry, even if you are a male.

If you would rather talk with someone about the issue, reach out to someone for help. Contact someone you can trust. You can write your thoughts and feelings down in a journal. The key here is to release all that is causing you to feel this way. Once you do this, you need to pick yourself up, brush yourself off, keep on going, and do not look back. You will get stuck if you dwell on it. Believe there will be brighter days ahead. You are not the only one experiencing times like this, trust me. If you or someone you know is facing problems that seem overwhelming, it is critical to get help immediately before reaching a crisis point. Please take advantage of the resources listed in the back of this book or use the Internet to research a specific concern.

Attitude

Do you have a positive attitude? You have complete freedom of controlling your attitude. A positive thought process and a positive mental attitude go hand in hand and will bring you happiness and success in life. It is important to maintain this type of approach at all times, not just when you are feeling it. A good habit that will change your life is to practice self-awareness. Stay positive even when negative situations arise. It is not healthy to be pleasant one minute and evil the next like in the story of Dr. Jekyll and Mr. Hyde. Yes, there are days when you feel more upbeat than others, but always maintain a positive attitude. Everything will work out as it should.

If someone is behaving in a negative way, do not let him or her drag you down. Just noticing the negative attitude is a step in the right direction. Be optimistic and stay on top of things. If the person says something negative, I know it is much easier to agree with him or her. But if you honestly do not agree, being silent is the better way to handle the situation. If you feel the need to contribute to the conversation, say something positive. The challenge here is to be optimistic and to generate positive energy. This will be a test for you, because there are many people who are ready and waiting to tell you "their stories."

Intelligent people can be rude and impatient with people who take longer to complete a task or have difficulty comprehending something. Instead of being critical of slower people, help them along, encourage them, and show them how to do the job. Just because you are bright and can pick up on things quickly does not necessarily mean you will be successful and happy. You also have to know how to interact with people and have compassion. Southern Baptist leader Mr. Zig Ziglar wrote this: *"Your attitude, not your aptitude, will determine your altitude."*[24] In other words, you will go farther in life with a positive approach.

Control

Nobody likes to be controlled. Period. Have you ever tried to control someone—a spouse, boyfriend or girlfriend, friend, child, or whomever? Have you ever noticed that when someone tries to make *you* do something you do not want to do, you become defensive and maybe even do the opposite?

God created us to be happy and to be able to make choices based on our own free will. When you try to control other people, you will only get frustrated. The only person you have control of is yourself, and you should not let other people control you. You are very capable of making good, sound decisions. You are in control of your own life. No one else is, unless you give them permission. The best thing you can do in life is to concentrate on controlling your thoughts, words, actions, and emotions. When you can control yourself and be responsible for your life, any situation will take care of itself. In fact, if you really want to control someone or something, you can by *not* being controlling.

---

[24] BrainyQuote.com, accessed August 29, 2014, http://www.brainyquote.com/quotes/quotes/z/zigziglar381975.html

What makes you believe your thoughts are right when another person believes something different? That is why we have control issues. Not everybody thinks the same way as you and sees things as you see them. We always believe we are right, but in reality, nobody is right, and nobody is wrong. You have to learn to let go of whomever or whatever you are trying to control. So why put yourself through all that frustration? Things usually have a way of working out, and besides, it will only be a matter of time before the situation changes again.

Do not complain about other people and what they are not doing for you. They are living their lives according to what they want to do. I am sure you do not like being manipulated. When you help other people, you will get the help you need. Appreciate whatever anybody does do for you. Do not *expect* people to do things for you. You are setting yourself up for disappointment. Do it yourself, hire someone to do it, or do not do it all. We tend to expect people to be the way we want them to be, instead of who they really are. Love and respect them no matter what.

This next part is for parents. Sometimes parents control their children to the point that they become rebellious when they grow older. This is when they are struggling to be who they are and not who you want them to be. We all want the best for our children. I know it can be difficult for a parent to sit back and let a child make mistakes, but this is how the child learns. When you are constantly doing everything for your child and giving him or her everything, how is your child going to learn to accept responsibility for him- or herself? You have probably heard this before: "Do as I say, not as I do." You will have greater success teaching your child if you intentionally *be* the person you want your child to grow up to be. This technique has more impact on a child's life than any other method.

We have many debates over religion, politics, religion versus science, etc. The main issue that causes these debates is control. The government and religious leaders impose their opinions on people in order to gain control of the people. We must abide by the government's rules and regulations, but at least we have options with religious beliefs.

The same thing goes for controlling situations. You will get aggravated when you try to control every single event in your life or in other people's lives. Certain situations are beyond our control and will occur as they should. If it is not what you wanted or expected, you still have to accept it for what it is and believe there is a greater power working behind the scenes for you. You must have faith and trust in this power and roll with it. That is all you can do. Accepting what is does not necessarily mean you have to say yes to everything when it comes to making choices. This is a common misunderstanding. You are accepting what is instead of trying to change what is *already* happening. You will experience more peace by surrendering to what is. When you do have to make a decision, be conscious so that you will make the right one.

Judgments

Do you make judgments about other people? Are you quick to judge someone you do not even know based on his or her appearance or behavior? That person could be the most thoughtful, loving, kind person you would ever want to meet. You cannot judge a book by its cover.

It is impossible to make an accurate judgment about somebody. Even if you know the person, you should not judge him or her. You are not them, and you have no idea what might be going on in their lives. You may think you know by their behavior or by the way they look, but your thoughts can deceive you. You do not know their circumstances, so it is best to stay out of their business and focus on your own life. Do not expect everyone to be like you and never assume anything about anyone.

Even if we know people are doing the wrong thing, sometimes we need to let the cards fall where they may. Who are we to judge? It is difficult to walk in someone else's shoes. Be caring and compassionate by talking with them and offering your help and support. You can provide help and guidance to a certain point, but they have to want to help themselves. They need to learn to take full responsibility for their own lives.

People judge other people according to their race, color, gender, sexual orientation, religion, nationality, profession, political beliefs, etc., due to their own insecurities. When you say something negative about someone, take notice, because it is actually a reflection of where *you* need to improve in life. What you observe in the other person is also in you. It is your subconscious letting you know you should be correcting your own behavior. You should judge no one. Criticism can take many different forms, such as analysis or constructive criticism or critique, which are acceptable ways to provide technical feedback. Being critical of people because of personal opinion does not work for a good life. God created all of us to be different. You should evaluate yourself on what, where, why, and how you could improve your life.

We are physical forms, and these physical forms come in many diverse shapes, sizes, textures, and colors. The purpose of our physical forms is to house the most important part of us which is our inner being or the core of pure consciousness. The inner being is the part we all have in common; it gives us our deep connection to the creator of this universe. When you are tempted to judge another by appearance, keep in mind that the part you need to identify with is the inner goodness within the physical form of that person. This is the part that is exactly the same as what you possess.

Complaining, condemning, and criticizing people will only affect you. You will get back what you generate. Would you want someone treating you that way? You cannot change the person, but you can change yourself. Be more accepting of that person for his or her inner goodness. You never know what that person is going through. When we criticize other people and then say, "Just kidding," that does not work either. Your words reveal your thoughts. You cannot take back the negative comments you have already spoken. This is the most appropriate quote for this topic: *"Be sure to taste your words before you spit them out."*[25]

Never accuse anyone of anything. You do not always have all the facts, so how can you be so sure this person did this? If there is any doubt about what someone tells you, stay neutral and ask questions before jumping to a conclusion. Put yourself in the same position. How would you feel if someone accused you of doing something or saying something when you were totally innocent? Some people think they know it all and are quick to point fingers, because they are clueless about life.

Also, never tell people they are wrong. You have the option not to agree with them, but it is not your place to correct someone. You can say you feel differently about whatever is being discussed. Everyone is entitled to his or her personal opinions. Besides, you may come to find out that you are sadly mistaken. In situations like this, it is best to think twice before you speak. It is better to be loving and kind than to be right.

If you judge other people, you probably judge yourself. To overcome this, you have to disassociate yourself from negative thoughts. When you notice you are criticizing yourself, say something positive and uplifting. Know in your heart that you are truly good enough and capable of achieving many great things in life.

Competition

I know all you athletes, sports fans, beauty pageant contestants, etc. may not agree with me on this one, but here goes anyway. Competition causes negative energy, tension, and conflict. Life is not a contest. In order to become successful, you do not need to defeat anyone. You may be smart enough to know how to defeat your opponents, but you are wise when you know you do not have to. We are all talented and beautiful individuals. When you want peace and

---

[25]   Author unknown

security in your life, you will have to avoid competing with other people. Your only competition should be with yourself. If you have a need to win, win with yourself and win at life!

I learned this at a younger age when I was a member of a swim team. It was a wonderful experience when I would win a race. I loved all the excitement and recognition, the blue ribbons, and the pats on the back. On the other hand, losing was very difficult for me. I would get so upset with myself even though I practiced hard and did my very best. I was not only letting the team down, but I was also letting myself down. Soon I became discouraged and felt I was not good enough. Remember, since we are all one, and we are all connected, when you compete with someone else, you are also competing with yourself. Each one of us has many diverse talents, yet we are all the same.

Competition is a way of satisfying the ego by showing the world who is the best. The ego wants all the attention and glory, and winning a competition provides this. It is always concerned about what other people think. The ego has you believing that if you win, you will gain power. However, when you become attached to results and the need to win, you will be disconnected from the true source of power. When someone comes along and does better, you will lose your self-confidence, and feelings of failure and disappointment will set in. We will experience downfalls in life that will help us evolve, but not from trying to gain recognition from people. We need to focus on being creative and productive and seeking God's approval. We need to figure out what our assignment in life is from God.

There is sibling rivalry in many families, but brothers and sisters should not compete against each other (love you, Tony and Alexis). We are in this together, and we should work as a team to love and support each other. We are all on this journey together we call life. Instead of competing with each other, we should be helping and uplifting each other to become the best we can be. We are all winners; we just have to realize it.

Chapter 6

Overcoming Peer Pressure

Do you feel like you are under a lot of peer pressure? Peer pressure is sometimes the cause of problems for the younger generation. Just to be cool and be in the "in" crowd, do you say and do things you normally would not do? Well ... forget that! This is serious stuff.

If you are in a circle of friends that is gossiping about someone, you can contribute to the conversation by supporting that person, or you can simply drop out of the conversation and walk away. Instead of putting someone down, we are supposed to be supporting him or her. Do not agree with what your friends say or add to their comments if it is something hurtful. Do not let them suck you into the drama. Put yourself in the person's shoes they are judging and imagine you are the one they are criticizing. How would you feel? People can be cruel. Avoid drama like the plague. Whenever you feel uncomfortable about any given situation, obviously it is not right. You must make your own choices and do the right thing.

Make your decisions based on what you believe and not on what someone else says. You do not need to follow what other people do, because it is not always the right thing. Remember this: misery loves company. Let your intuition be your best guide. Your intuition can save your life. Do not worry about what other people think, and do not worry about pleasing others. There is only one person you need to please and that is yourself. Instead of being a follower, strive to be a leader and teach people what you know about life. Teach them how to make wise decisions. Encourage them to follow their own hearts instead of someone else's. Here is a famous quote by religious leader and influential public speaker, Mr. William J. H. Boetcker: *"That you may retain your self-respect, it is better to displease the people by doing what you know is right, than to temporarily please them by doing what you know is wrong."*[26]

There are people who think they are way too cool to change. But really they are the ones who should be examining themselves to figure out where they need improvement. When your life gets tough, are those people going to be around to help and support you? I do not think so, because they need all the help they can get for themselves. But let me tell you one thing: your friends will really think you are awesome when you have it all, and you are on top of the world!

Alcohol and Drugs

Substance abuse will put you on the wrong path in life. Alcohol and drugs such as marijuana, cocaine, prescription pills, etc., sold for nonmedical purposes are used as a temporary fix to escape reality. These substances can cloud a person's perception and alter their minds to the point where they are not their normal self. Their state of mind can cause them to do things they typically would not do, such as lying, cheating, stealing, etc. Excessive consumption makes it difficult for a person to function properly. It affects their behavior in such a way that they can become very aggressive and physically violent. A person's physical form is also affected in a negative way from alcohol and drug abuse.

Alcohol and drugs can overtake your mind completely and can cause serious damage to an attractive, healthy body. Your body is strong but not indestructible. This process happens so gradually that

---

26   Values.com, accessed August 19, 2014, http://www.values.com/inspirational-quotes/3130?page=39

you are not even aware of it, and pretty soon you become addicted to whatever you are using. Finally, your body becomes immune to it, so you will need more of it. You have to have it to feel good about yourself. You will do whatever it takes to get your fix. You will try to hide the things you do wrong. You will have no appreciation for life. Once you are addicted, it is very hard to break this habit. To prevent any of this from happening, please educate yourself on the abuse of alcohol and drugs and what it does to your life. Your life is in grave danger if you are mixing alcohol and prescription pills. It could lead to death.

Have you ever been out with some friends and ended up at a party or place where people were doing drugs? The best advice I can give you is to leave immediately. If you did not drive your car, get a friend to take you home, or call someone to come and get you. If you stay, you may be tempted or persuaded to try "something" just to be cool. You may say to yourself, "Oh just one time will be okay. It is no big deal." That is all it takes to wreak havoc in your life—just one time. So here again, be in the present moment so you will know what to do when temptation arises. You will have the willpower to say no if you are placed in an uncomfortable situation. Stay away from alcohol and drugs. Hang out with the *right* crowd and not necessarily the "in" crowd.

As life goes on and you continue to use drugs, it will become harder and harder to quit. Help yourself right now and tell yourself that you want to quit. Do not wait any longer. Do it today for you. I know you can do it, but you have to want to do it. We should let our minds and bodies only be controlled by our hearts and intuition. Life is definitely worth living, but only you can determine that for yourself.

When all else fails, and you truly want to help yourself, reconnect with God (or whatever you call the entity or source from which you were created). Ask for help. You will receive the power, strength, and love from the source to overcome the hardships you are experiencing. Do not be stubborn, because it is impossible to do it alone. Do not worry about how you are going to do it, but trust and believe with all your power that you *can* and will do it. When you reconnect with the source, miracles will happen. Please reach out to someone who can help and support you. Talk to a parent, friend, coworker, or someone else in whom you can confide and to whom you can open your heart. There are support groups and drug and alcohol rehab treatment centers available to assist you. To get you started, here are some websites that offer support and will guide you to the right direction based on your needs and where you live:

- www.recoveryconnection.org
- www.nida.nih.gov
- www.samhsa.gov
- www.drugfree.org
- www.addict-help.com

Although alcohol is legal, be advised that there are legal ages for drinking alcohol in all countries and states. To find out the legal drinking age for where you live, you can go to this website: http://en.wikipedia.org/wiki/Legal_drinking_age.

If you notice a change in someone that is not good, confront that person to see if you can find out what is causing the change. Offer to help him or her. If you or someone close to you is addicted to drugs or alcohol and a child is involved, please ensure that child gets the proper care he or she needs. That child is just beginning in life and needs much love, attention, and guidance. It is unfair for an innocent child to live in unhealthy conditions. You would not want that child to grow up doing the same thing. People with these addictions are in a state of unconsciousness. They are not their true selves. They are not aware of their behavior and how they are affecting the lives of others. Some addicts finally wake up after hitting rock bottom, but some never wake up. Do not wait to quit until it is too late!

Chapter 7

Accepting the Flow of Life

Let It Go

Letting go, or *Let it go*, is a phrase that is frequently used in today's society. What does "let it go" actually mean? Letting go does not necessarily mean to get rid of. When you let go, it means you are *releasing* thoughts about something or someone that you have become attached to. You are freeing yourself from the attachment. An attachment is when you are consumed with thoughts or feelings about a person, place, thing, event, situation, problem, etc.

It can be difficult to let go of an attachment. If you are constantly directing all your energy to the attachment, it will be even harder to let go and take longer for you to move forward in life. Letting go is when you surrender to whatever you are consumed by and have faith that everything will work out. Surrendering to life as it is currently is not a sign of weakness but a sign of strength and courage. Sometimes we try too hard in life and struggle when there is no need to. Life is very simple if we just let it be and go with the flow.

I listened to Dr. Wayne Dyer speak once, and he said, *"Be open-minded to everything and attached to nothing."* If you want to make big life changes, you have to be willing to let go of what you *think* you know. Some people think they are right all the time. When you are willing to admit that you might be mistaken about what you *think* you know, things will begin to shift.

If you are experiencing something negative in your life and you want things to be different, let your request be known, and then go about your daily activities. Letting go of the need to make things right immediately will reduce the pressure. Letting go will lead you to the path of peace and healing within and will allow you to become a stronger and better person. Thinking about it and talking about it will only delay the process. Direct your attention and energy to all the good things in your life or to something new. When you let go of something, you are handing it over to God. By doing this, you are putting your faith and trust in God. The Beatles got it right with their song *"Let It Be:"* [27]

> *When I find myself in times of trouble*
> *Mother Mary comes to me*
> *Speaking words of wisdom, let it be*
> *And in my hour of darkness*
> *She is standing right in front of me*
> *Speaking words of wisdom, let it be*
> *Let it be, let it be*
> *Let it be, let it be*
> *Whisper words of wisdom, let it be*
>
> *And when the broken hearted people*
> *Living in the world agree*
> *There will be an answer, let it be*
> *For though they may be parted*
> *There is still a chance that they will see*
> *There will be an answer, let it be*
> *Let it be, let it be*

---

[27] "The Beatles Lyrics: 'Let it Be,'" ABC Lyrics, accessed August 29, 2014, http://www.azlyrics.com/lyrics/beatles/letitbe.html

Let it be, let it be
Yeah there will be an answer, let it be
Let it be, let it be
Let it be, let it be
Whisper words of wisdom, let it be

Let it be, let it be
Ah let it be, yeah let it be
Whisper words of wisdom, let it be
And when the night is cloudy
There is still a light that shines on me
Shine on until tomorrow, let it be
I wake up to the sound of music,
Mother Mary comes to me
Speaking words of wisdom, let it be
Yeah let it be, let it be
Let it be, yeah let it be
Oh there will be an answer, let it be
Let it be, let it be
Let it be, yeah let it be
Oh there will be an answer, let it be
Let it be, let it be
Ah let it be, yeah let it be
Whisper words of wisdom, let it be.

When you desperately want something, the same method works for attracting something to you. Let it be known and then forget about it (law of attraction). If it has not happened yet, do not obsess over not having it. Let it go. As soon as you do this, you will see how soon it will come to you.

The same process applies if someone is interfering with your happiness. The key here is to be conscious so that you will be able to recognize who or what is causing you to be unhappy. You must make amends with anyone who has caused you pain and suffering, and let it go. Do it for you. Holding a grudge against someone is only hurting you. By letting go of the attachment to whomever or whatever, you will feel relieved, almost as if a big burden has been lifted from your shoulders. Why? Because you have given it to God to handle. Besides, God may have a better plan for you. When you set your priorities straight and no longer try to seek happiness from people or things, you will soon discover how easy it is to let them go. Wish them well (you will also get it in return). Here is what leading Buddhist teacher, Mr. Jack Kornfield, has to say about letting go:

> *Letting go is a central theme in spiritual practice, as we see the preciousness and brevity of life. When letting go is called for, if we have not learned to do so, we suffer greatly, and when we get to the end of our life, we may have what is called a crash course. Sooner or later we have to learn to let go and allow the changing mystery of life to move through us without our fearing it, without holding and grasping.*
>
> *Letting go and moving through life from one change to another brings the maturing of our spiritual being. In the end, we learn that to love and let go can be the same thing. Both ways do not seek to possess. Both allow us to touch each moment of this changing life and allow us to be there fully for whatever arises next."*[28]

---

[28] Jack Kornfield, "Did I Love Well," excerpt of *A Path with Heart—A Guide Through the Perils and Promises of Spiritual Life*, accessed August 29, 2014, http://www.yin4men.com/files/59265197c5c5c28b45e5f3b50eeccc2f-143.html

Accept People

One of the biggest challenges in life is to accept people for who they are. When I am dealing with people (friends, family, coworkers, etc.) who are constantly negative and do not have a clue about life, I just want to shake them and tell them to wake up and that life can be really good. I get frustrated after I have talked to them about being optimistic and what I know for sure about life, but it just does not sink in. They are probably reliving their pasts and are unaware of their thoughts.

There have been times when I had to walk away from these types of people so that I would not *react* to all the drama and negative comments. I respect and love them dearly, so the way I tolerate their behavior is to focus on *the good* in them. I know they have kindness in them, because at times it peeks through their negative attitudes. I have to tell myself not to give up on them, because at one point in my life, I was struggling too, so I feel the need to help them. Most importantly, we must accept them for who they are at the moment.

We do not know what is going on in other people's personal lives that may be affecting their behavior. We may only know a small portion of everything. When we do not have all the facts, we need to seek to understand before we make any judgments. Change the subject when there is a disagreement and talk about something positive and encouraging.

There are so many people in this world who are struggling with their thoughts and fears and are unconscious of their behavior. People make their own choices in life, and whether those choices are right or wrong, it is none of our business. We can encourage them, but we cannot get discouraged, especially when we know they are making a mistake. When someone close to you changes, accept him or her for whatever the changes are. This will prove your love, compassion, and friendship toward people in this stage of their lives. Their experiences are an important part of the awakening process, and they must figure it out for themselves.

Another point I would like to make is to be careful not to lose your strength when it comes to dealing with difficult people. It can be very easy to agree with them and fall back into the same old negative patterns. I have found myself doing this just to stay friends with people and so that they would still like me. In actuality, this type of behavior is not what I am practicing and encouraging. When I realize what I am doing (and I thank God when I do), I say something positive, choose to remain silent, or walk away. By setting a good example, I am confident that they will want to naturally react the same way. I have to *be* the example I want so desperately to see in them. Be firm and stand up for what you believe, but at the same time, do it in a gentle, loving way to gain respect from others.

Once again, we must accept people for who they are without trying to change them. Nobody likes to be controlled by us telling them they need to change. Do not get me wrong. Change is a good thing, and people need to change to better themselves, but they have to want to change. This kind of change has to come from within. Nobody else can make them change. You can encourage people to make positive changes in their lives, and you can be a good influence for them, but they have to want to do it. We can be there for them, guide them in the right direction, and continue to help them along the way. We can provide the love and support they need while doing so, but they have to do it themselves.

Have you ever heard the saying, "You can lead a horse to water, but you cannot make it drink?" Do not get upset when you try to help someone and he or she is not willing to change. That person has to find their own way. We can help people out of a ditch, but they will probably fall back into it. But when they can do it on their own, they will probably stay out of the ditch.

We cannot change others, but we can certainly change ourselves. If you would like to see the world change, you have to *be* the change you would like to see in the world. Here is a little prayer I love, and is accredited to Mr. Reinhold Niebuhr. The best-known form is this one: "*God, grant me the serenity to accept the things I cannot change, the courage to change the things I can, and the wisdom to know the difference."*

Accept Yourself

How would you describe yourself? Is it the real you, or are you wearing a mask? Who is underneath that mask? Have you ever wished you were someone else? It is an uneasy feeling to be constantly evaluating ourselves to see how we compare and measure up to others around us. There are people who are never satisfied with who they are or what they have in life. And guess what ... those people may be wishing they were more like you, believe it or not. What you see and find so attractive in others must also be in you; otherwise, you would not see it.

The first step to self-improvement is to fully accept and appreciate who you are. Self-acceptance is when you accept your *authentic, real* self (the essence of who you are) rather than who you *think* you are or should be. Your sense of self-worth is the single most important determining factor for happiness, abundance, and good health. Your self-worth is not dependent upon other people's acceptance of you. There is no amount of self-improvement that can make up for the lack of self-acceptance. I have concluded that one reason why we may have difficulty in accepting people for who they are is because we have not yet accepted ourselves for who we are.

You were created perfectly, although at times, you may have contradicting thoughts about this. But those thoughts are not who you really are. Your job is to rise above those thoughts and declare that you are whole. When defining who you are, the first two words should be "I am" followed by a positive adjective. These two small but very powerful words are stating a fact that is already true. You need to proclaim it to yourself, especially when those negative thoughts creep in. When you say these words with emotion and enthusiasm and *believe* them, you will see how quickly your life will change. Here are a few examples of what I am: I am happy, I am strong, I am at peace, I am healthy, I am powerful, I am love, I am beautiful, etc. The list goes on and on because I am a wonderful human being, and so are you.

Focus on your strengths to activate more of them within you and become confident and determined to achieve your desires. Self-acceptance is essential for evolving and becoming the person you are meant to be. Why not start right here, right now, and accept you for you and all the fine qualities and talents you have and have always possessed?

Here is a good positive affirmation written by Mr. Thich Nhat Hanh: *"To be beautiful means to be yourself. You don't need to be accepted by others. You need to accept yourself."*[29]

Accept Current Situations

There are many times when we will be disappointed in life, when things do not go according to our plans. We must choose to respond to these situations in a positive manner. Accept change without getting upset or frustrated. There will always be changes; some are natural and some unexpected. When things are not what we expect them to be, let things flow naturally. There is no point in trying to force things to happen.

Do you know what it is like to swim against the flow of fast-moving water? I know for sure that it is hard work and a struggle. Well, the same thing happens with the flow of life. When your plans do not work out and you resist what is happening, you end up working twice as hard. Instead, you must change your direction and move along with the flow. Life will be a lot easier and much less stressful.

Believe that whatever is happening to you now is only temporary, and there will be brighter days ahead. The more you struggle with

---

[29] "Thích Nhất Hạnh > Quotes > Quotable Quote," Goodreads. com, accessed September 25, 2014, https://www.goodreads.com/ quotes/350914-to-be-beautiful-means-to-be-yourself-you-don-t-need

the situation, the longer it will take to pass. Keep smiling knowing that you are in control of your destiny. As much as we want things to always work out positively, sometimes they do not, so why dwell on it? We need to get over it and *let it go*. When we become stuck in one area, we need to shift our focus onto other areas.

I know it can be upsetting when things do not always turn out the way we want them to. But in order to have happiness in life, we have to accept whatever is going on at the moment. It has to happen this way, so have faith that you will eventually get what you want (remember the law of attraction). You may not get it right away, but be patient and you will see how everything plays out at the end and why everything happened the way it did. It may be even better than you expected.

Instead of complaining or getting angry, be accepting of the present moment, because it is already happening. When you resist what is happening, you suffer pain and anxiety, so why fight it? You just have to let go of the need to control the situation. Keep in mind that you will get what you want because God wants us all to have a very easy, simple, and happy life. We are the ones who make it seem so difficult. God always has the perfect plan for you. Once you see the positive results, you will come to realize that things happen in perfect order. In all situations, we must keep the faith, accept it as it is, and believe with our hearts it is happening for a very good reason. It is wonderful when our plans work out, but if they do not, accept what is, because either way, it is a win-win situation.

CHAPTER 8

Changing for the Better

"You must be the change you wish to see in the world."
—Mahatma Gandhi

Change Within

Change is constant, and everything can change in the blink of an eye. Do you embrace change, or do you reject it? There are people who are perfectly content staying in their comfort (safe) zones and where they are in life. They are afraid to make changes, because they fear the unknown and are skeptical of the outcome. Change is good, whether it works out or not. We have to learn to take that step of faith. Taking risks will help build our confidence, provide more opportunities, and help us overcome the fear of failure. The lessons we learn from failure may put us on a new and better path.

You can choose to shift your life at any time. For me, this book is living proof of major changes in my life. The most important point I want to make in this section is this: when you want to discover more about yourself and improve your life and be happier, you have to work from the inside out. This means you have to first become aware of your inner being and what you are thinking and feeling. By understanding your thoughts, you can change them and how you react to certain situations. Positive energy will bring you positive effects.

Your mind is so compelling, and what you think, you bring into action. It has to do with the law of attraction we talked about earlier. As you think a certain thought, you are attracting that object or energy to you from the universe. It works the same way for attracting people and actions. There is no such thing as a coincidence. Remember that because we are all connected, our minds are all joined together. So whatever situation you are in right now, the good news is you can choose to change it. You have to want to change, take control of your life, and make your intentions good.

Have you ever experienced a wake-up call? And, no, I do not mean a phone call from the hotel's front desk to wake you up at a certain time. I mean something drastic that has happened to you that was extremely unpleasant and not expected, perhaps like a car accident, health issue, etc. This is God tapping you on the shoulder and telling you to snap out of it (be more conscious, pay attention, be mindful) and realize that perhaps you need to make some positive changes in your life. You will receive many signs from God, but you have to be aware of them.

When these unpleasant things happen to us, we cannot get mad, wonder why they are happening, and blame everyone else but ourselves. Instead, remind yourself that it could be a sign from God, nudging you to examine yourself to determine what is not currently working in your life and why. It is God's way of encouraging you to become more aware of your thoughts and actions and to take control of your life. When you ignore the signs, the pain and suffering could get stronger until you get to the point where you cannot stand it anymore. This is when you could be thrust into an awakening. Challenges can also set you back and push you into a deeper state of unconsciousness. That is why when you experience hardships, it is important to realize you need to take a good look at yourself to see where you can improve.

If you are currently experiencing negative feelings about your life, you can choose to change. If you are sad, angry, discouraged, depressed, etc., do not just sit there complaining about it and acting like the victim. You have got to do something about it. I am confident you can do it. You made choices that put you in your present situation, so you can make choices to turn things around. You can make up your mind to change your life, but *you have to really want to change.* It may sound like a lot of work to you, but trust me; it is worth every effort you put forth. There are four words that begin with the letter "d" that are vital for making a permanent, healthier lifestyle change: desire, discipline, determination, and dedication.

Anything you do consistently becomes a habit. We have good and bad habits, as I talked about earlier in Chapter 1. Bad habits are sometimes a result of negative thoughts and could include judging people, gossiping, complaining, criticizing, eating too much, abusing alcohol and drugs, etc. If you have a few bad habits, you still have the opportunity to correct them. You can improve the quality of your life right now by changing bad habits. The longer you wait, the more challenging it can become. People with a positive thought process usually practice good habits. Healthy habits include loving and respecting yourself and others; practicing gratitude; being kind, humble, and compassionate; etc.

I have been working on a habit I have had for a very long time. My obsession is trying to be perfect in everything I do. Do I try to achieve perfection for myself or for other people? I feel like I have accomplished something when I do it perfectly. Since it is only a temporary state, this causes frustration and unhappiness. I am choosing to let go of the need to be perfect all the time. I am focusing on progression and excellence, and I am enjoying life more. We live in a world where we are allowed to be imperfect.

Be aware of your thoughts and habits. Self-awareness is the key to success and positive development. Self-awareness is important for living a truly satisfying and peaceful life. Make every decision with a conscious effort, and you will choose well without regrets. Best-selling author Mr. Eckhart Tolle said this: *"You suddenly find there's another dimension deeper than thought inside you.*[30] Here are a couple more things you can do to change for the better. You need to take some type of action to change any situation. When you want your dreams to come true, take action. Start by being honest with yourself so that you can be honest with other people. You can speak up, be honest, and tell people exactly how you feel or what is on your mind (in a respectable manner). You can choose to accept what is going on in your life at the moment (but do not complain about it). Appreciate your life for what it is and consider other options to make it even better. Remember, you have the power within you to change anything about you. When you stress and worry about something, the issue will continue to annoy you. Once you make a decision, whether it is right or wrong, do not look back. Let it go and believe everything will work out for you. Trust in the decisions you make for yourself and then move forward. If at first things are not working for you, hang in there. You will be so glad you did. Be strong, confident, and keep the faith. I am telling you that things will eventually work out, even if it does not go the way you planned.

Step out of your comfort zone, be original, and try something new or seek different ways of doing things. Experience new foods, change your hairstyle, change colors in a room, or take a different route to a destination. Perhaps you will find that you like the new way better than the old way because it is easier, faster, or more scenic. A new hairstyle can completely change your appearance. And yes, sometimes change is not always the answer, but how will you ever know without trying it? I love change. I am willing to try new things, and if it works out for me, great! If it does not, I can at least say I tried and that maybe it was not meant to be. If it is something I really desire, I will continue to experiment with it until I know for sure, and just maybe I will get better results.

---

[30] "Creating a New Earth Together," Oprah talks to Eckhart Tolle, by Oprah, O Magazine, Paragraph 13, eckharttolle.com, accessed January 30, 2015, http://www.eckharttolle.com/article/Eckhart-Tolle-Oprah-Winfrey-O-Magazine-Interview

Believe in Yourself

Why is it so difficult for some of us to accept a compliment? Do you feel uncomfortable when you receive praise and approval and lots of attention? There have been times in my life, when I would actually deny a compliment. Was it because I felt I did not deserve it or was not good enough? When someone gives you a sincere compliment, do not brush it off. Accept it, absorb it, run with it, and be grateful! Thank them for reminding you that you *are* beautiful and you *are* good enough. Believe in yourself, because you will become what you believe

This is what Ms. Joyce Meyer has to say about loving yourself: *"Don't be overly concerned about what other people think of you because it is what you think of yourself that matters the most anyway."[31]* Be kind and gentle with yourself, just as you would treat a newborn baby. You have to take care of you and be grateful for who you are. Do yourself a favor and give yourself a special treat. What is the most wonderful luxury you can give yourself? Do it today, because you deserve it.

Tell yourself that you are a great person and that you can achieve great things, and *believe* it! When you realize that you can do anything and think positive thoughts, miracles will happen! Remember, whatever you think, you create. There may be struggles along the way that are meant to happen to possibly lead you in a different direction, but have confidence in yourself. When you lack self-confidence and always doubt yourself, you will end up following someone else's path.

I cannot tell you enough that you have to believe in yourself and trust that the world is right. When you believe in yourself, you believe in God. What brings joy to your life? In order to get what you want in life, you have to believe you will get it without any doubt. I can say with certainty that if you believe with positive

---

[31]   *The Wisdom of Making the Right Choices,* Joyce Meyer Ministries, accessed September 25, 2014, https://www.joycemeyer.org/Content/Downloads/bootcamp_the_wisdom_of_making_right_choices.pdf

emotions (like when you believed in Santa Claus) and get excited about life and know that God has all these wonderful things lined up for you, you will get everything you want and more.

It baffles me that on application forms (particularly for employment), we often have to complete specific questions regarding our race (classification system used to categorize humans), gender (the state of being male, female, or intersex), marital status, culture, ethnicity, nationality, etc. and other questions based on our past (e.g., criminal conduct is considered in determining suitability). People are people—not categories. These types of questions can be discouraging and intimidating and prevent us from having faith in ourselves. We all mess up. Everyone deserves a second chance. Does it make a difference *what* we are? The application process should be based on *who* we are (skills, attitude, abilities, talents, ethics, etc.)

Did you know that con artist and impersonator Mr. Frank Abagnale committed numerous crimes but was later hired to work for the FBI? Mr. Abagnale served time but was granted parole by the United States when he was twenty-six. In exchange, the government told Mr. Abagnale that he had to educate them about his methods so that they could prevent others from defrauding the government. In fact, a movie was made based on the life of Mr. Abagnale titled *Catch Me If You Can*, starring Mr. Leonardo DiCaprio. [32]

I want to prove a couple of points here: 1) if you made some bad decisions in the past, now is your chance to turn your life around, and 2) even if you have committed a serious crime, you can still apply for any job, including government. So get rid of the excuses. (I wrote this part for someone who I love and respect. You know who you are.)

Be confident in yourself and what you can accomplish. God created a wonderful, talented human being, and you should love, respect, and honor yourself as such. When you have faith and believe

---

[32] "Frank Abagnale Jr.," A&E Television Networks, accessed July 30, 2014, http://www.biography.com/#!/people/frank-abagnale-20657335

in yourself, things will turn around for you. Mr. Neil Gaiman summed it up perfectly in a commencement speech to University of the Arts graduates: *"But the one thing that you have that nobody else has is you. Your voice, your mind, your story, your vision."*[33]

Respect

It is important to have respect for all life. Respect is a feeling of admiration, and showing high regard for someone. Do you show respect and consideration for other people and their opinions? Learn to respect people of all ages and levels of responsibility. Do you have respect for yourself? Be a good role model and respect yourself and appreciate all your fine qualities. You will earn the respect of others and maintain many good personal relationships.

Signs of respect for other people can be as simple as holding the door open for someone, shaking hands, or by saying "God bless you" after someone sneezes (which originated in Rome years ago from the belief that a sneeze typically precedes illness).

Do you respect the person(s) you live with? If you are still living at home or sharing a house or an apartment with a spouse or roommate(s), the following questions pertain to you:

- Do you think you can just take someone's possessions without asking permission first?
- Do you immediately replace the items after using them?
- Are you conscientious about taking care of whatever you borrow?
- Are you tidy, and do you keep your space organized and clean?
- Do you offer help with whatever needs to be done inside or outside the home?
- Do you automatically empty the garbage when it is full?

---

[33] The University of the Arts, Neil Gaiman: Keynote Address 2012, accessed on February 3, 2015, http://www.uarts.edu/ neil-gaiman-keynote-address-2012

- Are you considerate when it comes to noise?
- Do you pitch in with buying food and other necessities?
- If you are a man, do you put the toilet seat down after you are done in the bathroom?

To keep peace and harmony in the home, these are all things to consider. Kindly ask the other person if you may have or borrow the item you need, and assure them you will replace it or return it in the same condition. It is important to be considerate of the other household members. Would you want them to take your things and not replace them, ruin them, or even lose them? Be fair about replacing food items, especially if you are sharing expenses. Share responsibilities with cleaning, grocery shopping, paying bills, etc. Always be respectful toward each other.

Gratitude

Are you a grateful person? Do you appreciate everything God has done for you, the gifts you have received, and all the beauty that surrounds you? Gratitude is an absolute must! Sometimes when we have everything we want, we become ungrateful and do not appreciate what we do have. We should be very grateful for what we have and not complain about what we do not have. Remember, it can all be taken away very quickly! We should not only go to God when we need or want something, but we should thank God every single day for our blessings and appreciate everybody and everything. A good habit to get into is to write down ten things you are grateful for every day. I keep a gratefulness journal, and oftentimes I will write with my emotions.

I am sure you have heard this saying before: "You do not know what you have until you lose it." That is a good lesson for all of us. People could lose a loved one, their wealth, etc. at any time. Do not wait until something bad happens to appreciate things. Perhaps if that person comes back or your financial situation improves, then maybe you will learn to be more grateful. When things do not work out, be grateful anyway for whatever God has in store for you. You may be guided to someone or something better. Do not take people for granted. Let them know and show them that relationships are important to you. People will want to do more for you and give you more if they know you sincerely appreciate them. When you have some free time, it is always nice to send them a note, text, e-mail, etc., acknowledging your friendship and gratitude and thanking them for being a part of your life.

When there is something you really want or need, without any doubt, have faith in God that you will get it. Be grateful for it before you even get it, and act like it is already on its way. Give thanks and you will receive it. Before I get out of bed every morning, I thank God for that day and every day of my life and for guidance and help throughout the day. Every day I repeat, with sincere gratitude and appreciation, a few small phrases to myself: thank you for the healing of my mind, thank you for the healing of my lips, thank you for the healing of my heart, thank you for the healing of my soul, and finally, thank you for the healing of my life.

When you are truly grateful for what you are and what you have, you will end up being more and getting more. Gratitude will get you what you want. Be grateful for all that you are every day of your life, even when you do not succeed at something. Everything will work out just fine. God wants you to be happy and to have the absolute best life possible. When you wake up each morning, before your feet touch the floor, smile and say to yourself, "Thank you, God, for this glorious day and every day of my life. Please give me the guidance I need for today."

Forgiveness

Do you find it difficult to forgive someone? Has someone close to you ever hurt you mentally or physically and you just cannot seem to forgive that person? How can we forgive someone who has caused heartache and pain? How can we forgive someone who has committed a horrific crime? Forgiveness is letting go of resentment and anger toward that person. Forgiveness is letting go of the need to get even, and releasing negative thoughts. Holding a grudge will only cause you pain and suffering. Forgiveness frees you from the past and is for your benefit. Being the better person trumps falling into his or her same behavior pattern. Remember, we all make mistakes. You owe it to yourself to forgive. Do it for the love of life.

We must forgive our enemies. Remember, if we are all God's children, they were also created with love and have love in them. They just do not know it is there, but we do, and that is why we must forgive them for whatever they have done to offend you. They were unconscious or unaware of what they were doing at the time. The Bible says to "*forgive them, for they know not what they do*" (Luke 23:34). As spiritual teacher, Mr. Eckhart Tolle interprets this to mean they were not in the *present moment*. They were too caught up with their negative thoughts and emotions. You could say they were not spiritually connected with the source. We must forgive them anyway.

The following is a short story I would like to tell you. My daughter, Sarah, and I went to a home improvement store to purchase porcelain tile flooring. I went to the service desk, and a younger man immediately offered his assistance. I was surprised but then I suddenly wished someone else was helping us, because this man was rude and abrupt from the very beginning. It took all my power to remain calm and not complain. My daughter also recognized that he clearly was not himself. After telling us what we needed and how much, he walked away. Sarah actually stacked six boxes of tiles onto the flatbed cart for me. She said she would rather do it herself than ask for his help. When we were driving home, we talked about this man's behavior. My daughter reminded me that he could be going through a rough time in life. Although he did not live up to my expectations, the man was doing his job from his level of awareness. I accepted this man for who he was at the time. The next day, I contacted the department store and, much to my surprise, did quite the opposite of what I would have normally done. I actually recommended that this man receive some type of recognition for his service. This is called forgiveness.

Besides forgiving other people, you also must forgive yourself. No matter how well you treat others, there may be times when you hurt someone unintentionally. Do not beat yourself up over it. When you are humble and admit your mistakes, you will be forgiven too. We have all made choices we regretted later, but do not dwell on them. Instead, see it as an opportunity to change. When you have negative thoughts about yourself or someone else, do not listen to them. Forgive yourself for judging anyone. Forgive yourself for whatever wrong choices you have made in the past. Forgive yourself for the mistakes you have made. Forgive yourself for failing. Forgive yourself just like you must forgive your enemies. You are a great person. It is time to be strong and be confident and move on. You were created with love, so find the love within you to forgive!

Generosity

Are you a generous person? When do you feel really good about yourself? I bet when you look your absolute best, you feel confident and proud of yourself. What makes you feel really good on the inside? Giving something to someone or doing something for anyone is a rewarding experience. Be generous and give from the heart because when you give, you will receive. When you put fruit in someone's empty basket, your basket will be kept full. Life is all about giving and receiving.

Since we are all connected, we should want to help and support each other and be kind and considerate to everyone. Doing the right thing always makes us feel good on the inside, and this is when you are aligned with the greater source. If you are searching for ways to feel good about yourself, here are just a few examples: give someone a compliment and really mean it; open the door for someone; help someone with anything; give someone a gift even if it is small; share your knowledge; donate something to charity like old clothing; or throw some extra change in the Salvation Army bucket during the holidays. There is a whole list of ways to feel better in the "Happiness" section in Chapter 4.

Giving, no matter what or how much you give, makes you feel good about yourself. Be generous and give from your heart. When you give something to someone or do something nice for someone, do not expect something in return. When you do this, you are doing it out of the goodness of your heart, without expecting the other person to return the favor or give something to you. A good experiment would be for you to remain anonymous when you are giving. If you expect something in return, you will only be hurt or disappointed if that person does not reciprocate. Be a good example for everyone else by being a giving person. Have you ever heard the expression, "Pay it forward?" This means when someone does something good for you, you turn around and do something good for someone else. Instead of paying back that person, you are "paying it forward" to the next person.

My mom was the most generous person I know. She was constantly donating to charities whether it was money, food, clothing, household items, etc. If you visited her at her home and told her you liked something, she would want to give it to you. She would rather give away what she had than buy something new for herself or her home. My mom loved to cook and bake and take food over to the neighbors. She was always treating other people to breakfast, lunch, or dinner. I am honored to call her my mom.

Random acts of kindness are a wonderful way to show your consideration and compassion for other people. Although some people perceive kindness as weakness, in actuality, it is strength that many people lack. Perhaps they feel that when you are kind you want to gain something in return, or you have no set boundaries and you are basically a pushover. People who think like this are usually the ones who are insecure and lack ability in their own lives.

My daughter, Sarah, is also a very generous person. She is always throwing money into a donation bucket or basket. One year, she and I wanted to do something special during the holiday season. We decided to randomly do acts of kindness. We visited a nursing home, and we bought gift certificates and handed them out randomly to people we did not know. It was fun to see their reactions. Some people were even hesitant to accept the gift. Ms. Oprah Winfrey is an awesome gift-giver! I watched her show when she revealed her "favorite things." She gave everybody in the audience things she favored. I remember another time when she gave each audience member a car! Wow! She is a true inspiration to all of us and such a generous, caring person!

When you want to make someone else happy, it would be so nice to give that person what *he or she* wants if at all possible. Just because you like something does not necessarily mean the other person is going to like it. Go out of your way, ask questions, be a good listener, and take the time to find out what that person would really love to have. Guys are usually into technology, and you cannot go wrong with giving a woman a piece of jewelry. Naturally, we should always be appreciative and grateful when receiving a gift no matter what it is.

Okay, so if you do not have the money to buy something, make something or offer your help. Homemade items are more meaningful than items purchased from a store. Older people living alone would really appreciate any help you can provide. Mow the grass, shovel snow off the driveway, rake leaves, pick up groceries, etc. Go visit the elderly in a nursing home. Show them there are caring people in this world. They only want your companionship which does not cost you anything except some of your time. It will be time well spent. You may want to listen to them carefully because you will probably learn something. I used to do some volunteer work at an elementary school, because I love being around children. They are so innocent, always happy, and full of life. It was such a rewarding experience.

It feels really good when you help people and when you are kind and generous and offer your services. When you start to feel pressured into doing something, it becomes stressful. You have to look out for *numero uno* and take care of yourself, especially when you are being pulled in too many different directions. This is not about being greedy or selfish. Sometimes people will take advantage of a good thing, and they have to figure things out on their own. If someone is constantly relying on you for help, it is okay to say no if you honestly do not feel like doing something. Do not feel guilty about it. You can let that person know in a kind way that you care about him or her, but you cannot help them this time. A good friend should understand that you have options too. If he or she gets upset with you, it is okay. You are not going to please everyone. Practice pleasing yourself.

My daughter, Sarah, is a very kind person and is always willing to help whomever with whatever. There are times when she really does not want to participate in doing something but feels bad if she does not. She is afraid people will get mad at her or talk about her. She needs to get over the fact that she is not going to please everyone. She has to learn to say no without worrying about what other people think or say. We need to create boundaries in our lives. We have to learn when to say yes and know when to say no without letting it bother us. If you are not happy doing something, do not do it! You are not obligated to do anything when you do not feel good about it. You will feel drained, overwhelmed, and unhappy. You will be miserable if you continue to do things you do not enjoy doing.

Honesty

Do you tell the truth? Do you know how important it is to tell the truth ... all the time? If you are a dishonest person, it will be hard for you to trust others. You will be constantly wondering if they are being truthful (remember that karma thing again). When you tell the truth, you will feel good about yourself, and other people will trust and respect you. You, in turn, will be able to trust other people. The truth is always easier to maintain than a lie. You can never slip up on the truth. Honesty is the best policy.

Be honest even if you know it might not be the answer someone wants to hear. I have always been a compassionate person. When it comes to telling people something I know might hurt their feelings or offend them, I want to avoid being straightforward with them. There have been times when I said things that were not necessarily true so that I would not upset them, but that is being dishonest. Yes, it may be a small white lie, but it is still lying. Many of us have a need for acceptance. Knowing what is expected of us, we pretend to be what people want us to be, but then we are not being true to ourselves.

I would like to share with you a little lesson that I learned. A good friend of mine gave me a gift card as a Christmas present one year. Instead of buying something for myself, I used it to buy a birthday present for my oldest daughter, Chelsea. My friend kept asking me if I bought anything with the gift card, but I did not want to tell her how I spent it. I avoided the subject, because I was afraid she would be offended. I kept telling her that I had not bought anything yet. One day she asked me again, so I finally told her exactly what I did with it. She was upset with me and explained why. She was more bothered by the fact that I was not being upfront with her than me buying something for my daughter.

Although the truth might hurt at first, people will love you more when you are totally honest with them. Of course, you do not have to blurt out to someone that you do not like their hairstyle or shirt or whatever. When someone asks your opinion, be truthful but in a kind way. You can say something like the other shirt looks better or the other hairstyle is more becoming. You can also assure them that it is what they like best that matters most. Encourage people to feel confident about making their own decisions. If ever you are put on the spot, there are ways around it without being hurtful or disrespectful.

If you are a trustworthy person, people will confide in you. It may take time and patience to earn their trust. If someone tells you something in confidence, be respectful of that person and keep the conversation to yourself. Listen, offer your support if needed, and let that person know he or she can confide in you. If you want people to put their trust in you, you must trust them as well. You will live a happy life if you can trust other people. If you tell the truth all the time, you will have nothing to fear. Being a dishonest person can be exhausting because you have to keep up with all the lies. If you are a deceitful person, you can be guaranteed you will eventually get caught in your lies.

I always thought there were two sides to every story, but I met a new friend who once told me that there are three sides to every story: your side of the story, the other person's side of the story, and of course … the truth!

Chapter 9

Promoting Good Health

Good health is not just the absence of disease. It is the state of complete mental, physical, social, and emotional well-being. Well-being is our sense of how well, satisfied, and contented we are with life.

Inner Being

I bet you feel good about yourself when your hair looks nice, your clothes fit just right, and you are happy with your appearance. Yes, you should always take care of your physical self, but you should feel good about yourself no matter what. Many people believe if they are beautiful and good-looking, they will be happy. True happiness comes from what you are feeling within your body. The physical part of you is a reflection of what your thoughts and feelings are. When you are happy on the inside, it will show on the outside. You will feel confident about yourself and love yourself solely for who you are.

To achieve beauty on the inside, you must have a pure heart; always stay positive; be loving, kind, grateful, generous, forgiving, and faithful; and accept everyone for who they are and every situation for what it is. To attain all of this, you should live in the present and enjoy each precious moment as if it is the only moment. Constantly be aware of your thoughts, actions, and everything that is happening around you so that you make the right choices. This is how you achieve natural physical beauty, but it is the inner part of you that really counts. Life is grand, and when you are a beautiful person on the inside, your love of life is reflected on the outside.

Appearance is not as important as personality, character, or behavior, and you should not base your thoughts on what you see. *You can walk confidently in public with an attractive partner, but you will live happily ever after with someone who has a kind heart and is pure in spirit.* Society dictates that you have to be good-looking and thin to be happy and successful and to enjoy life. Yes, there are many attractive people who are happy and wealthy, but there are also many handsome men and pretty women who are unhappy. You would think they would be very happy with their good looks, thick hair, slim and toned bodies, etc. Right?

Happiness comes from within our physical forms, from our state of mind, from our spirit, and from our hearts. You can make many physical changes to the outside of your body, but it is the inner part that will determine your happiness. You have to love yourself for the way you were created and know that your thoughts are not the real you. Your thoughts could lead you to believe that you are not pretty enough or good-looking enough. You must turn those thoughts into positive ones. If you want to have a wonderful life, look within and figure out what you can do to become a better person. Here is a great quote by Ms. Helen Keller: *"The best and most beautiful things in the world cannot be seen or even touched. They must be felt with the heart."*[34]

Balance

Having balance in your life is very critical for having a happy, healthy lifestyle. Too much of anything is not good for you. You do

---

[34] "Helen Keller > Quotes > Quotable Quotes," Goodreads. com, accessed September 15, 2014, http://www.goodreads.com/ quotes/4900-the-best-and-most-beautiful-things-in-the-world-cannot

not have to go to extremes or get too intense to enjoy life. Balance your life with work and play. All work and no play is not good. Get your mind off work and enjoy other activities or hobbies life has to offer. However, all play and no work is not a balanced lifestyle either. You cannot sit around and watch TV all day long or hang out with friends 24-7. It is time to get ambitious and do something creative. You will feel so much better when you accomplish something in life and have something to show for it.

Balance is critical in a working environment. If you currently have a job, the work must be balanced. You must pull your weight in a job and not expect other people to do your work for you. Constantly working overtime and obsessing over your job is not good either. If you are working too hard and never have enough time to do fun things, it is time to make a change.

Some highly educated and extremely intelligent people can be too serious at times and do not know how to interact well with others. These types of people need balance in their lives. It is good to be well educated, but it is just as important to have fun and laugh a lot. This would help them to loosen up, get out of their thinking minds, and divert their attention to the outside world.

You also have to have balance in a relationship. All relationships, including spouse, partner, family, friends, co-workers, etc., have to have balance. Balance is the key to making any relationship work. It cannot always be a one-sided affair. It is natural for every one of us to want attention and affection, but we must also show the same toward our counterparts. It cannot be one person constantly putting forth all the effort in a relationship. Eventually that person will become exhausted from trying to make things work in the relationship. Appreciate each other and do not take advantage of a good thing. You do not know what you have until you lose it. It takes fifty percent from each person to maintain a balanced, healthy, and happy relationship. Pitch in and help each other, no matter where you are or what you are doing. Ask if there is anything you can do for the other person.

For the female role: You have to step up and do your part. We all like to be wined and dined, but it works both ways. We should show our love, appreciation, and respect for our partners too. If living separately, offer to drive to his apartment or house. Cook a good dinner and offer to help with the chores.

For the male role: At one time, females stayed home and took care of the children and did all the housework. It has completely changed nowadays. Women have careers and work full-time jobs too. Men, you have to pitch in with caring for the children, the housekeeping, and whatever else needs done.

You must also have balance in dieting and exercising. You should eat with awareness and choose healthy foods to stay fit and strong and to get the nourishment your body requires. It is all right to indulge in dessert or something fattening once in a while, but you should not overdo it. Definitely do some type of exercise during the week. If you want to have a perfectly balanced schedule, you can exercise three and a half days per week.

We talked about spirituality earlier. Both the spiritual and physical parts of our human existence play a critical role in our well-being, and balance between the two makes us whole, complete, and healthy.

Physical Being

The human body is the physical structure that houses our inner parts that function to give us life. What you look like on the outside is an indication of what you have been feeling on the inside. A healthy mind creates a healthy body. Do you feel healthy and full of enthusiasm?

There are people who believe illness is hereditary, and that may be true in some cases, but you can also create illnesses through negative thinking and emotions. Since we know for sure that negativity causes health issues, why not stay positive to stay healthy? When we are facing difficulties in life, we can overcome them with positive thinking, strength, and determination. Remember, we have the power within us to move mountains (not physically, of course, but with a positive mindset and optimism). How healthy you think you are is how healthy you are going to be.

What is your body telling you? Listen to your body, because it does not lie. Your body will react to certain situations and give you warning signs. Be aware of them. Usually when you get sick, it is your body's way of telling you to slow down, rest, and examine your thoughts. Negative thoughts can definitely cause health problems. Worry, fear, stress, anxiety and the feelings of insecurity are some of the major causes of sickness and poor health. If you can recall, were you angry, upset, or worried about something days before you became ill?

When you are experiencing minor aches and pains, perhaps your body is trying to tell you to reprogram your thoughts. Do me a favor. Stick it out for a few days and give yourself time to recuperate. Be optimistic that you will get better, and focus on how healthy you are. The body has natural intelligence with the capability of healing and repairing itself. Healing herbs and/or other natural home remedies can be as effective as traditional treatments. If the problem persists, by all means, get examined by a medical professional.

Note: if you are suffering from any chronic mental, emotional, or physical disorders, seek the advice of a physician or a medical professional immediately. If you are currently taking any medication prescribed by your physician, continue taking it according to the directions from your doctor or pharmacist, and follow-up with your physician. Always contact a physician or qualified health care provider if you have any questions regarding a medical condition. The information provided in this book is solely for education and is not intended for professional medical advice, diagnosis, or treatment.

Rest is essential for maintaining good health, especially when you are going through a change in your life. Change could cause emotional anxiety. The best thing to do is get adequate rest to refresh and recharge your mind, body, and spirit. Climb into your nice comfy bed and go to sleep. Calm your weary mind from all the thoughts going through your head. If you feel tired during the day, take a nap, even if it is for only fifteen or twenty minutes. Rest will replenish the energy and strength you need to push forward and approach change in a positive manner.

I feel great after sleeping well and giving my mind and body a good night's rest. When I wake up, I feel reenergized and ready to deal with life's challenges. You probably have heard this expression before; it has been around for a while. It was written by Mr. Benjamin Franklin: *"Early to bed and early to rise, makes a man healthy, wealthy, and wise."*

When we are facing obstacles in life or dealing with change, sometimes we tend to keep busy doing things just so we do not have to think about them or deal with them. If we overexert ourselves with activities, day after day, week after week, we could experience more problems, such as exhaustion and stress. Meditating or taking a walk helps me to relieve stress and think clearly about issues. Sometimes it is good to sleep on it too. However, you do not want to sleep constantly or fall into depression. We talked about balance earlier, so you should know when you are ready to resolve the problems. Resting and relaxation are great remedies for clearing the mind and healing the body.

In addition to being a positive person and getting proper rest, you should practice good hygiene, eat healthy, and exercise to keep your body healthy and the energy flowing. Good posture is a sign of strength and confidence. You should always sit up straight and stand with your shoulders back and your chin up. We must take care of our bodies.

To achieve an optimal state of health and well-being, a healthy diet is the first step. Eating the right foods (and portions) can help you sleep better, provide more energy, and help you think more clearly. Fruits and vegetables are the perfect foods for providing vitamins and nutrients. When you crave a specific food, it is your body's way of telling you that you need certain nourishment. Go for it and eat whatever you are craving (especially if you are pregnant). Here is another good quote to follow by Mr. Benjamin Franklin: *"Eat to live, don't live to eat."* According to Mr. Robert a Schuller and Mr. Douglas Di Siena, you can *"add years to your life and life to your years"*[35] in their guide for spirit, mind, and body which encourages readers to exercise regularly and eat healthy.

---

[35] Robert A. Schuller and Douglas Di Siena, *Possibility Living: Add Years to Your Life and Life to Your Years with God's Health Plan* (New York: HarperOne, 2002)

CHAPTER 10

Maintaining Relationships

Here is the suggested hierarchy to follow for establishing lifelong relationships. Your primary relationship should be with God. God should come first in your life since God is the source of all love, all power, and all supply. God will deliver the strength you need and the will to become the authentic you so that you can help yourself and other people. God is your number one fan.

The most important person in your life is you. You are with you 24/7. There is no escaping you. You will do more things for yourself in life than anyone else. It is necessary to attend to your needs so that you are better equipped to provide the support and care for others who will be part of your life. So impress yourself. You have to have a loving relationship with yourself first in order to attract loving and lasting relationships with others. Your inner self will determine the types of people you will attract. When you have peace and contentment within, you will attract kind and gentle people to you. Surround yourself with positive people who love and support you. They will help you grow to be your best possible self in any relationship.

Your spouse or partner should follow next and then the children (if you are a parent). Your spouse or partner is there to support you in life, especially during trials and tribulations. Sometimes we put our children before our spouse or partner, which can cause problems. Your spouse or partner is also there to help you with raising the children. He or she might have some positive contributions that you may not have.

Following thereafter would be your parents or guardians, in-laws, and the rest of your family, relatives, friends, co-workers, etc. There are exceptions to rules, but in general, this order will provide you a good foundation for sustaining healthy, caring long-term relationships.

Many different people will come into our lives. Not everyone is going to impress you at first, but if you seek out the best qualities and characteristics of that individual, it can develop into a healthy relationship. There are three types of people that will come into your life: people who need your help, people who are on the same path and have the same outlook on life, and people who will help you. When you have some leisure time, you should hang out with people who are on the same path and who will help and support you. This way, you will be able to enjoy your free time without the stress of work.

Another important suggestion I have about relationships is that you should always be your natural, beautiful self with everyone. When you want to be happy, you have to be yourself. Be proud of who you are and your own unique creation. Do not try to conform to other people's wishes or desires and who they want you to be, because you will get tired of it. When you are your authentic self, people will love you for who you are, and you will have peace in life. The following quote was written by the late Ms. Debbie Ford and relates to what I am encouraging you to do: *"The greatest act of courage is to be and to own all of who you are—without apology, without excuses, without masks to cover the truth of who you are."*[36]

If people want to be in same-sex relationships, and it feels natural to them, then that is their business. They know how they feel and

---

[36] "Spirituality Practice, Resources for Spiritual Journeys," Spiritualityandpractice.com, An Excerpt from Courage: *Overcoming Fear and Igniting Self-Confidence* by Debbie Ford, accessed February 3, 2015, http://www.spiritualityandpractice.com/books/excerpts.php?id=22716

what they want to make themselves happy. We are not them, and we are not living their lives, so why should we interfere? We need to concentrate on our own lives and figure out what makes us happy. We need to love them and everyone else for who they are, no matter what. (I wrote this part for someone very dear to me. You know who you are. Love you.)

Connection, communication, compromise, and commitment are essential for establishing healthy, lasting relationships. Both parties must contribute to building a strong relationship. The key to a satisfying relationship is keeping the lines of communication open. Express your ideas, desires, concerns, and beliefs with each other and learn to appreciate and accept the differences. Compromise and work as a team and cooperate with each other. We are not incapable of doing things alone, but when our ideas, talents, and abilities are combined, we can create wonderful and meaningful things together.

For a relationship that needs repaired, figure out what *you* can do to make things right. You have to learn to change yourself. Not all people are meant to stay in your life, especially if you are experiencing change. Those people may no longer be at the same place as you are. We cannot expect people to be who we want them to be. We will become very frustrated with the relationship. They have to want to change for themselves. Some people will change and some will not. Either way, we must accept them for who they are.

Take your time before making any rash decisions. Work things out if possible, because there will be issues in all relationships. Communicate and be open and honest with each other. The best way to deal with conflict is to confront every issue as soon as it arises so that it can be resolved as quickly as possible. Unresolved conflict festers. Keeping something inside does more harm than good. How does the other person know what is wrong if you do not tell them? Be calm and discuss the problem without screaming or yelling at each other. Listen carefully to what each other has to say. Attack the problem, not the person, and focus on a solution.

Whenever you feel uncomfortable in any type of relationship, whether it is a family member, friend, or a loved one and you know something is not right, you need to communicate your feelings with that person to resolve the issue. There should never, ever be any kind of force or violence in any relationship. When you cannot resolve the problem, it is best to let someone else know about it, because your thinking can be unclear at that point. Confide in someone you know and trust and who will help and support you. There are many good reputable professionals who would be willing to help you with any kind of issue. Please refer to the "Online Resources" page provided in the back section for additional help and guidance.

Attraction

We are constantly attracting people into our lives. When we want to attract the right people, we have to first be right with ourselves. How can we be better so we can have better relationships? By being more loving, accepting, and supportive of ourselves, we can then provide the same in our relationships.

We talked about the law of attraction earlier in Chapter 3, "Understanding Your Mind and Thoughts." The law of attraction works the same way as when you are seeking a partner. For those of you who are not in a relationship but would really like to meet someone special, let it be known to God the kind of person you are seeking. To be very clear about it, make a list and write down all the qualities about the person you want to meet. Go about your business. I suggest you keep yourself active and do not obsess over finding a partner. Enjoy doing activities, meeting new friends, and learning new things. Before you know it, that special someone will appear in your life when you least expect it. Perhaps one of your friends will introduce you to the right person. You could possibly meet someone at school, work, grocery store, concert, or wherever, but I do not recommend going to bars. The people who hang out at bars are usually not themselves, if they have been drinking.

It is good to consider someone you *need* rather than someone you *want* (as long as you know who and what you need). When we get what we want, it satisfies us for a while and then eventually we will be looking for something else, and the pattern repeats itself. This philosophy works the same with relationships. Look for that special someone you *need* so that he or she can teach you what they know and help you to become more knowledgeable in those subjects. Be with someone who brings out the best in you. Both you and the relationship will grow stronger, and your life will become more balanced.

Do not depend on anyone to make you happy. If you are looking for that special someone to make you happy, look within yourself. Happiness comes from within, and that is where you will find it. The same goes for security. You cannot depend on a relationship for security. You will gain a sense of security when you have high self-esteem and faith in yourself and what you believe.

If you want the fairy tale and live happily ever after, look for a partner with strong core values over physical attraction. Pleasures of the body and ego and are not as important as one's character and beliefs about life. Find someone who inspires you to become the best you can be. Be aware that it works both ways. You must possess ethical values as well so you can inspire your partner into evolving and developing into his or her highest possible self. Here are some examples of ethical values: respect, integrity, excellence, authenticity, responsibility, courage, compassion, trustworthiness, fairness, etc. A healthy relationship will experience both pleasure and growth. Find someone who will love and respect you and lift you up.

Keep in mind that not everyone is like you. We are all unique. Do not try to please everyone; you will only be disappointed. If they do not like you, it is because they are probably not happy with themselves. Remember, like energy attracts like energy. You will attract people to you who are like you, and they will appreciate you for who you are. We are nourished by other people. There are so many people waiting and wanting to meet us. Get excited and enthused and be grateful for whoever may cross your path.

Dating

Are you going out with someone? Dating is a wonderful and exciting experience. Being in love is an amazing feeling! If you are dating someone, you manifested this person into your life. You attracted this person to you because you two were having similar thoughts and experiencing the same type of lifestyle. Life is great!

When dating, at first we are usually on our best behavior because we want to impress our partner. We will go to great lengths to do what it takes to get his or her approval. This is good, but we need to learn to be our natural selves, because how will we know if he or she is the right one? In every relationship, there will be differences. Can you live with these differences? If you do not know what they are, I suggest you take your time and get to know this person. Do not rush into anything. Find out what his or her likes and dislikes are. We should always be considerate and respectful of the other person, and it should never be one-sided. A good, healthy relationship takes balance. No one should be dominating the relationship. Meet halfway, give in to the other person once in a while, and go to the movie or restaurant of their choice.

If you are arguing and fighting all the time and cannot work things out, perhaps it is time for you two to separate for a while. Being away from each other will help clear your minds and appreciate the person you once admired. You may want to seek counseling. An unbiased person will listen to both parties and may be able to help you to remedy the situation. If there is any type of physical, verbal, or psychological abuse involved in a relationship, I highly recommend that you talk with someone about it, and get help from a trained professional. In the back of this book is a resources page for further assistance.

Commitment is a promise of trust, loyalty, and devotion to making the relationship work. We must put forth effort in keeping relationships. The easy way out is to walk away, but to work things out and overcome obstacles will sustain the relationship and make it grow stronger. If at any time during a relationship someone begins to change, you have to determine whether or not you can live with that change and accept and support the person who is changing. This is when the relationship can become challenging, especially if the change is not good. As much as we want our relationships to work, some just are not meant to be. You should not have to force anything that is truly meant to be. Deep in your heart, you know whether or not this person is right for you.

If you are dating someone and it has to be a secret, you should question the relationship. There should be no excuses and absolutely nothing to hide in any relationship if you expect it to last. It should be an open, honest, and trusting relationship.

Why does such a wonderful and powerful thing called love sometimes end so quickly? Instead of moving on in anger, resentment, and bitterness toward one another, you should thank that person for loving you and helping you realize that you are one step closer to the person you are destined to be with. It is better to have loved and lost than to have never loved at all. We do not own anyone but ourselves, so we should not become attached to anyone. When you try to possess someone, he or she will move farther away. The one and only attachment we should have is with God. God will always be there for you. A more positive note about all endings is that there are also new beginnings. One door closes and another one opens.

Intimacy

Did your parents ever explain to you the intimacy part of a relationship, or did you hear it from your friends? Typically, when two young people are in a relationship and are supposedly "in love," the natural thing they want to do is engage in sexual intercourse. If you are expecting fireworks and bliss, you may be disappointed. Immaturity and inexperience are two major factors.

Be advised, if you are a young person and your partner is older than you, there are legal ages of consent for sexual activity in all countries and states. They may be different depending on where you live. If you are uncertain what the legal age of consent is for your location, please be sure to research this information for your own benefit.

Being intimate with someone is a natural act and part of the human experience. When you start exploring each other's body, keep in mind that one thing may lead to another. When you are going to have sexual intercourse, please take the necessary precautions and be sure you understand the repercussions. Here are some important factors and questions to consider:

- Do you love this person? Are you doing it for you or your partner?
- Can you trust this person? Some people will tell you what *you* want to hear.
- Females are taking a risk with getting pregnant. What if an "accident" happens? Can you deal with the consequences? Bringing a child into this world is a *huge* responsibility.
- Some people are not ready to be committed to one person. What if you break up?
- There are risks of contracting sexually transmitted diseases.

Listen to your values and what you know to be right. If you ever feel uncomfortable in a relationship, stop, do not go any further, and do not lead your partner on. Trust your own instinct. It is usually right!

Sexual intimacy can be a wonderful experience and a life-changing event, but it is up to you to discover this and when. Making love with a partner is a celebration of life, and it should be a very special experience for both of you. It is important to get to know each other first and to be patient. Your hearts and minds must be in tune. Communicate with each other and spend time together. Visit with each other's families and friends. You will know whether or not this person is right for you.

Waiting to have sex until you are married is something to consider. Maybe this would make a difference in the divorce rate and marriages would be more successful and fulfilling. Premarital sex has been viewed as wrong and disgraceful, but then once the couple is married, they consummate their marriage by having sexual intercourse. It is no surprise when people have mixed emotions and feelings about sex after they get married. If you are having sexual intimacy problems, you have to break free from your conditioned mind and thoughts from the past and understand that it is a beautiful and loving experience. You may want to seek counseling from a professional who will help you with these issues.

Sexual intercourse can be for reproduction or just pleasure. As with anything, you should not abuse a wonderful and natural thing. Here is a great quote written by Ms. Marianne Williamson: *"The purpose of an intimate relationship is not that it be a place where we can hide from our weaknesses, but rather where we can safely let them go."*[37]

Promises and Trust

Are your actions aligned with your words? We all say we are going to do this and that ... but when it comes down to it, do we really do what we say we are going to do? Words are powerful, and they have a huge impact in a relationship. Remember, once you say something, you cannot take those words back.

A promise is a commitment. The moment you make a promise, you are committed to doing what you said you would do. You must be careful when making commitments, because people are expecting you to follow through with them. It can be very disappointing when you repeatedly break your promises. People will not trust you and eventually will lose respect for you. How can people defend you or be there for you when they do not trust you? A relationship without

---

[37]　"Enchanted Love Quotes," Goodreads.com, accessed September, 17, 2014, https://www.goodreads.com/work/quotes/398021-enchanted-love-the-mystical-power-of-intimate-relationships

trust is difficult to keep. You must make every effort to fulfill your obligations.

Sometimes we make promises to people even before thinking about them, and due to certain circumstances, we cannot fulfill them. I know you want to do whatever you can for that person, but some things are beyond our control and are not meant to take place. However, some people do not understand this. The key here is to be aware of what you are agreeing to do. Take your promises seriously. If you agreed to do something for someone, you must honor your word. It is all about taking action. Here are a few meaningful quotes relating to this topic: talk is cheap; actions speak louder than words; talks a big talk (brags a lot but never follows through); and, as Mr. Benjamin Franklin said, *"Well done is better than well said."*[38] Do you get my point?

Having good intentions is great, but action should support what you say. A word of caution: before you make a commitment to anyone, be absolutely certain you can and will fulfill that commitment. A man of his word (also a woman of her word) is someone you can trust. Trust is the glue for all relationships. *"Trust takes years to build, seconds to break, and forever to repair."*[39]

Do you ever make promises to yourself, and do you take them seriously? It is equally important for you to keep the promises you make to yourself. It takes discipline to do this, but then you will also be able to keep your promises to other people.

Expectations

In the section above, we talked about people having high expectations. Is it good to have high expectations of yourself and other people? It is good to live up to the quality of life you want, as long as it is what you want and not for the purpose of pleasing others. Reasonable

---

[38]   BrainyQuote.com, accessed September 17, 2014, http://www.brainyquote.com/quotes/quotes/b/benjaminfr103731.html

[39]   Author unknown

expectations of yourself can be a positive effect on your life provided that you stay balanced. I have very high expectations of myself, and when things do not work out for me, I have to remind myself to stay positive and confident. I still expect wonderful things to happen, knowing God is behind it all. Besides, it seems I am more grateful for the good things that happen unexpectedly.

Failing is God's way of telling us that we may need to make some changes, try other options, or walk away from it. At times I have felt like I let myself down because of my high expectations, leaving me insecure and discouraged. I have finally accepted the fact that it is okay to fail. Failure is good because it gives us strength and courage to move forward in life and on to bigger and better things. We will fail many times, so keep the faith. Smile when you fail because you will still succeed.

In addition to having high expectations of myself, I have always had high expectations of other people (especially people who are close to me). I have to be careful when expecting people to be like me, because I am setting myself up for disappointment. I have expected people to behave a certain way and be able to do certain things my way. I should only be accountable for myself. I was surprised to learn that a lot of people do not have all the answers or know how to do something (even though they may act like they do). High expectations of other people will diminish happiness. We should expect one thing from other people, and that is for them to be themselves, not who we want them to be. Yes, we are all connected through the same source, but each one of us was created with uniqueness. We must accept people for who they are and not who we *expect* them to be. Mr. Robert Fisher wrote, *"When you learn to accept instead of expect, you'll have fewer disappointments."*[40]

---

[40]　"When You Learn to Accept," livelifehappy.com, accessed September 17, 2014, http://www.livelifehappy.com/?s=robert+fisher

CHAPTER 11

Interacting with Others

Connection

A relationship is a connection and exchange between entities. I cherish every connection I make with another being. Connections can be in person, in writing, or through thought. As soon as my day begins, I connect with the number one entity in my life: God. I thank God for a new day and being alive and well.

Everyone has something to offer this world. Pay attention to everyone, because we learn from each other. We attract many different people into our lives consciously or unconsciously. By observing and/or listening carefully to others, you may be inspired by someone, or you may be reminded that not everyone is at the same level of awareness as you. Either way, be grateful for whoever crosses your path, because we are all a work in progress. My three-year-old grandson teaches me to be happy for no reason.

Many people will walk right by others without any kind of acknowledgment. I have noticed coworkers doing this while walking through the hallway. Some people walk with their heads down, looking toward the ground. They are probably lost in thought. A nice gesture would be to lift their heads up, and at least acknowledge other people by nodding, smiling, or saying hello. For goodness' sake, it does not take much to be kind. When someone asks how you are doing, tell them you are doing very well. Why would you not respond in a positive manner? At that instant, you are there, you are alive, and everything is all right. Nine times out of ten, people do not want to hear about your problems anyway. They are just being considerate. You should also be courteous and ask how they are doing because remember, it is not always about you. Keep your life balanced.

Making eye contact is when two people look at each other's eyes at the same time. Eye contact is a sign of confidence and demonstrates that you are fully focused on the other person. Sometimes we can communicate with our eyes without even having a conversation. The eyes are often referred to as *the window to the soul*. The eyes can tell us a lot about a person and give us clues as to what he or she may be feeling or thinking. When you see a twinkle or gleam in the eyes, that person is feeling happy. When people avoid eye contact or blink often, they may be feeling guilty or nervous about something. Eye movements can reveal the difference between love and lust. Feelings of love will show in a person's gaze into the other's eyes, and if the eyes wander below the face, there are feelings of lust. When there is a blank stare, that person may be bored and thinking about other things. Do me a favor. The next time someone is speaking with you, look directly at their eyes and give them your undivided attention. When you are driving, you can glance over at the other person periodically to make eye contact.

Anytime you come in contact with someone, acknowledge that person by name. Greeting someone by name is more personal and an indication that you were mindful when you were first introduced. That person will notice you made an effort to remember his or her name. Be certain of their name before addressing that person. If you are unsure, you can just say hello and that it was good seeing him or her. Acknowledgment is better than ignoring someone just because you do not remember their name, or even if you do not know the person.

Hugs are often a sign of affection and are nice to give people who are special. A hug transfers energy from one body to the other and adds meaning and warmth to the relationship. The next time you see someone you know, embrace him or her with a hug. By the way, the best way to give a hug is to put your arms around the person and rub his or her back with your hand in a circular motion rather than patting it. This gesture is more meaningful and sincere.

On a more professional level, when you greet someone, a good gesture is to shake his or her hand. Grip the person's hand firmly with confidence (not limply), shake it and tell the person how very nice it is to meet him or her (by name). A firm handshake is an indication of strength and power. Females, you too should shake hands just like the guys do!

Please be on time for whoever you are meeting or whatever event you are attending. No one likes to be kept waiting. You are wasting their time, and this indicates lack of consideration. If you are running late, at least have the courtesy to call the person to let him or her know you will be late. Plan your time accordingly and be on time.

If you are going to a job interview, be on time and prepared. Have all the necessary paperwork with you. Look presentable and dress appropriately. Wear clean, pressed clothing so you look neat and responsible. Dress for success!

Communication

Communication is an exchange of life energy. We, as human beings, can communicate with our thoughts, voices, eyes, hands, facial expressions, and bodies. Whatever type you use, effective communication skills are absolutely essential for all relationships. Communicating allows us to express our desires. Lack of communication can cause problems in a relationship. How would we work with our coworkers? How would we resolve issues?

Are you afraid to speak in front of a group of people? This has been one of my fears for the longest time. It is still not one of my favorite things to do. As long as I am knowledgeable and interested in the subject, I will confidently speak about it. Do you voice your concerns, opinions, and beliefs to others? I avoid conflict as much as possible. Many times I would agree with whomever about whatever just to prevent an argument and possibly losing a friend. I speak up now more than I ever have, especially when it comes to doing the right thing. I think about myself and what I believe rather than pleasing the other person.

I usually avoid topics that instigate debate, such as religion, politics, abortion, gun control, same-sex marriages, etc. Everyone sees things differently, and everyone is entitled to their own opinions and personal preference. I still respect people for whatever they believe, even if it is something I disagree with. Arguing with people concerning their beliefs versus my beliefs is a waste of valuable time and energy. If asked, I will give them my honest opinion, and that is about the extent of it. What is the sense of insisting that I am right if I want to keep peace and harmony within me?

You may ask how do problems get resolved if they are avoided. Well, a simple way to resolve world issues would be to include the public in the decision-making. Take a vote similar to the voting process used for electing a president. After all, world problems affect everyone, not just select government officials. I am a fair and logical person. I want peace and harmony for our nation too. The government could still manage the processes and procedures.

When you speak to someone on the phone, always be kind and courteous, whether it is someone you know or is a stranger. We get plenty of unwanted phone calls from solicitors, volunteers, etc. When you do not see the person face-to-face, it is easier to be discourteous. There really is no need to be rude or angry on the phone. If it is bad timing when you receive the call, simply do not answer the phone.

Remember, the other person on the phone has feelings too. He or she might be trying to make a living by selling a product. Volunteers are working at no charge to help other people. If you are not interested, genuinely thank them anyway and tell them to have a good day. They will remember you in a positive way. What I like to do is catch them off guard and tell them yes, I would like to donate or purchase whatever they are selling and be cheerful about it. They are always so grateful, and it makes me feel good to know I made their day. Here is the golden rule to remember: always treat others the way you want to be treated.

In this day and age, we do much of our communication through texting, e-mails, voice mails, social networking, etc. It is not necessary for us to physically see the other person we are communicating with, so it makes it much easier to express our opinions and concerns. I believe that if you would not say something to someone face-to-face, do not type it in a text or e-mail. I am referring to nasty-grams. Read it again before you click the *send* button. Would you want to receive an e-mail or text filled with anger? Have you considered who might read it and to whom it possibly will get forwarded? It may come back to bite you, and it could end a relationship or even a job.

Listen

Are you a good listener? Listening requires real engagement. Active listening is when you are actually absorbing what the speaker is saying. You demonstrate this by responding with action like nodding, using a facial expressions, leaning forward to hear better, etc. Crossing your arms may seem defensive. Make it a goal to listen attentively and absorb what is being said instead of merely hearing the words. You do not necessarily have to agree or disagree with them; all you have to do is listen. Being an active listener shows that you are thoughtful and respectful of that person for what he or she has to say. Give that person your undivided attention. Listen with an open mind and without judgment.

You may be totally bored with the subject, but listen carefully anyway. Be considerate even if you have no interest in it. Be courteous, and do not look around during the conversation. This is rude and indicates that you could care less about what that person is saying. Do not interrupt or respond until the person is completely finished speaking. There is nothing more unbecoming than when someone is already speaking and another person starts speaking during the conversation. Be patient and respectful and wait your turn. You would want the same respect while you are talking. You will have the chance to comment afterward. Sometimes a good practice to follow is to remain silent for a short while to digest the information.

Make eye contact with the other person to let the person know your attention is fully focused on him or her. Look directly into their eyes until he or she is done speaking. Provide feedback to the speaker, but do not always try to be the center of attention, and do not act like you know it all, because there is plenty to learn. Sit back, relax, and enjoy the conversation. You just might learn something new.

Laugh and Smile

Do you like to laugh and have a good time? I love to laugh. It is important to have a good sense of humor. You have to enjoy life and have a good laugh every once in a while. Keep your life balanced, and do not be so serious all the time. We have all had funny things happen to us. It is fun to laugh heartily, especially for a really long time, until your sides actually hurt. When you are done laughing, you wonder what you were laughing about in the first place. Kids are so amusing. My little grandson says and does the funniest things. He sure does brighten my day when we are together.

Abundant laughter brings joy and happiness into our beings and is food for the soul. Even if it is something silly, laugh out loud (instead of typing lol) and let all the positive energy flow. Usually, when we are feeling good it is easy to laugh, but it is equally important to laugh when we are feeling down. My favorite movies to see are comedies. The next time you need a pick-me-up, go see a funny movie. Laughter renews our spirit and helps us focus on the positive things in life.

Laugher is truly the best medicine for the mind, body, and soul. It is a great stress reliever and can burn calories. Laughter is good for any type of illness; as a matter of fact, it can help in the overall healing process. Laughter has been known to actually cure cancer patients. It is also beneficial for the recovery process. When you focus on good health and all the blessings in your life (anything other than the illness), you will feel better!

It is a popular belief that it takes more muscles to frown than to smile, but some experts disagree. They believe it takes fewer muscles to frown than to smile. It does not take much effort to smile. Do me a favor. The next time you are feeling a little down, consciously force yourself to smile. Thoughts of something funny that happened or something sweet and lovable like a puppy or a newborn baby should make you smile. Your facial expressions influence your mood and emotions. You can change your mood just by changing your facial expression. When you smile, the muscles in your face send a positive message to your brain. When you are talking on the phone with someone, smile because although the other person cannot see you, he or she can still feel it and hear it through your voice. Everyone benefits from your happiness and smile, including you. Smile today at someone and to yourself because you are great! When you are smiling, so is God.

Do you realize the effect you have on other people? Yawns are catchy and so are our moods. Laughing and smiling are contagious too, just like yawning. We automatically do whatever the other person does. Smiling at someone is a sign of friendship, peace, and tranquility. Have you ever smiled at someone who looked sad and then all of a sudden a big smile appeared on his or her face? You probably made that person's day just by your smile. Smiling is an indication that you do care. The next time you see someone who looks unhappy, get him or her to smile. Let that person know that life is good, regardless, and that everything is going to be all right. Something as simple as a smile creates peace in the world. Mr. Joseph Addison once wrote: *"What sunshine is to flowers, smiles are to humanity."*[41]

Laugh and smile and always maintain the childlike spirit within you. Tell a joke, do fun things in life, and enjoy acting like a kid again. Laugh, laugh, laugh! This is a great quote by playwright Mr. George Bernard Shaw: *"We don't stop playing because we grow old; we grow old because we stop playing."*[42]

---

[41] "Joseph Addison > Quotes > Quotable Quote," Goodreads. com, accessed August 15, 2014, http://www.goodreads.com/quotes/76178-what-sunshine-is-to-flowers-smiles-are-to-humanity-these

[42] BrainyQuote.com, accessed August 15, 2014, http://www.brainyquote.com/quotes/quotes/g/georgebern120971.html

Chapter 12

Simplifying Your Life

It has become clear to me that life is very simple. Some people believe life is so complicated, probably because they have too many things going on. When you are trying to do too many things at one time, your life will become chaotic. Parents will run themselves ragged dragging their children to too many activities. Children need to stay active to stay out of trouble, but to a certain point. Allow them to select one or two of the ones they enjoy most. Just because children are involved in all kinds of activities does not necessarily mean that they will excel in life. They could end up being a *"Jack of all trades, master of none."*[43]

Spend quality time alone, with your partner, and with your family. You do not have to be constantly doing something every minute of every day such as hanging out with friends 24/7. Eliminate activities that do not benefit your life and concentrate on the constructive ones you enjoy doing. Rushing around and going from one place to another only causes stress and anxiety. Slow down and pay attention to what you are doing, especially when you are driving! Have you ever driven to a place and wondered how you got there, because you had no recollection of actually driving there? Take time

---

[43]   *Wikipedia*, s.v. "Jack of all trades, master of none," last modified August 31, 2014, http://en.wikipedia.org/wiki/Jack_of_all_trades,_master_of_none

out from your busy schedules and appreciate the meaningful things in life. Stop and smell the roses.

Simplify your life. Get organized. Clean out your car. Declutter your room and closet. Get rid of old clothes or items you have not worn or used for a while and donate them to your local charity. Minimize the drama in your life. If you think drama makes life interesting, think again! Life can be exciting without it. Drama causes chaos and conflict and can damage relationships.

It is the simple pleasures in life that give us a sense of peace. The little things matter the most. Cherish the simple things like sitting down and enjoying a meal with family or singing your heart out in the car by yourself or with friends. Listening to music is a great way to release us from the grip of excessive thinking. The simple things can relieve stress in our lives. Take a walk, cook, read a book, take a nap, draw a picture, watch the sun rise or set, take a drive in the car, or meditate.

Nature

Everyone and everything was created by the same source. Therefore, we are all connected to the source by the same source energy. This source energy is in human beings, animals, trees, plants, etc. There are many forms of life in this universe. There are probably some that exist that we do not yet know about. A life-form is an entity or being that is living or alive. We happen to be in a human being life-form. Spiritual teacher Mr. Eckhart Tolle says, *"you don't have a life, you are life!"*[44] *Life is not something we own. It is something we experience.*

Open your eyes to the beauty God has given us. Do you enjoy the outdoors and nature? I enjoy being outside, breathing fresh air, and taking in all the beauty that surrounds me. When I was a child, I used to play in the woods behind my parents' home. I would

---

[44] "The Wisdom of Eckhart Tolle," Peaceful Rivers, accessed September 18, 2014, http://peacefulrivers.homestead.com/EckhartTolle.html

stay outside until it got dark. I loved climbing on an old fallen oak tree trunk and walking barefoot in the cool clear streams. I had fun picking wildflowers and giving them to my mom. Flowers are beautiful and are great gifts to give someone to lift his or her heart. I love this Chinese proverb: *"A bit of fragrance always clings to the hand that gives roses."*[45]

The four seasons—winter, spring, summer, and fall—are wonderful examples of the constant flow of nature. When you are outside, do you ever feel the aliveness all around you? The different seasons bring change in the weather and surrounding environments. When it is raining outside, I find it very comforting to listen to the rain hit the windows. I love to take walks at night when it is snowing. Everything seems so quiet, still, and peaceful. To bask in warmth of the sun is so relaxing it sometimes puts me to sleep. A cool summer breeze is always refreshing after spending time in the sun. The best things in life are free.

Animals are also part of God's creations, and so many animals bring joy to our lives. I believe animals are very close to God. They are unlike humans who sometimes allow their minds or thoughts to get in the way of their connection with God. Do you have a dog or a cat or any other kind of pet? Pets offer unconditional love and affection and are very faithful. They can be therapeutic for people. Pets can reduce stress and tension and help people with depression. Hey, did you know the word *dog* spelled backward is God? I have an adorable little Maltese dog named Oscar. He brings so much happiness to me and my family. He is there to greet me when I walk through the door every day. He is always so excited to see me. He acts as though I have been gone for days, even if it has only been a short while. Oscar loves me without conditions, and I love him just the same. We may not behave the same or have the same physical attributes, but we definitely have a spiritual connection. When I look

---

[45] "Book Review," Spirituality and Practice, accessed September 25, 2014, http://www.spiritualityandpractice.com/books/books.php?id=18576

at him closely, his eyes communicate with mine. One time, I played a blinking game with him. Every time I would blink, he would blink. We kept doing this for about five minutes. It was so funny. Oscar does this other cute thing. When he sneezes, I always say, "God bless you." He actually forces himself to sneeze maybe two or three more times. And each time he does, I say it again. He is my best friend. I love this next well-stated thought. The author is unknown: *"My goal in life is to be as good of a person my dog already thinks I am."*[46]

A tree is a living thing. Trees seem so peaceful and strong. They stand tall and erect through all weather conditions; rain, hail, sleet, snow, wind, clouds, and sunshine. A tree may lose its leaves, but no worries, the leaves will grow back during the appropriate time or season. Trees have a purpose. They provide beauty, shade, shelter, oxygen, and wood products such as paper, furniture, and housing. Some trees provide flowers, fruit, nuts, and maple syrup. Appreciate the trees.

Animals, insects, the sky, clouds, rain, oceans, rivers, fish, sun, moon, stars, grass, trees, plants, flowers, rocks, and all the creatures in the world are God's beautiful creations. God created all life-forms—nature, animals, and humans. Therefore, God is in everything that has been created. If God is in all life-forms, we are all connected! We should love and appreciate all that God has made!

---

[46] Author unknown

CHAPTER 13

Aligning with God

Spirit Within

We are spiritual beings having a physical experience. Did you know there is a holy and beautiful spirit within you? This is your inner being; the very essence of who you are. It is also called your soul, core, presence, life-force, power, consciousness, chi, etc. It is a separate non-physical entity that gives you the spiritual connection to God. Your inner being is the divine part of you that is your Godlike power. It is where pure consciousness exists which gives you guidance and insight to fulfilling your calling in life. When your spirit is disconnected from God, you will experience conflict and confusion in your personal life and with the rest of the world.

Here are some great quotations about spirit I enjoyed reading on Mr. Jonathan Lockwood Huie's website:

> *"The cleansing fire of Spirit*
> *consumes the troubles of this world.*
> *Feed your concerns to the fire.*
> *Breathe deeply and rejoice."*

> *"Honor your being,*
> *Release each and every struggle,*
> *Gather strength from life's storms,*
> *Relax into the arms of spirit."*

"When I see Spirit in everything, Peace is at hand."[47]

The outer, physical body is the temple that houses your inner being. A lot of people are more focused on taking care of their physical parts. But you have to take care of your inner self as well. You may not be able to touch your spirit, but you can feel it, love it, nurture it, and listen to it. Meditate to clear your mind of the constant thoughts and noise and purposely connect your spirit with God. During this connection, you will become aligned with God. You will feel a sense of calmness that will bring peace to your mind, body, and soul. This is one of my favorite quotes, written by Mr. Eckhart Tolle: *"Power over others is weakness disguised as strength. True power is within and it is available to you now."*[48]

My message to you is that no matter how tough life may seem or how difficult it gets, keep your spirit alive. Your spirit is the most precious part of who you are. Tap into your spirit. Let your spirit guide you to what you should say, what you should do, and where you should go and when. You will soon discover life is much easier than you thought.

Purpose in Life

Why are we here? Your life's mission is to discover who you are, why you are here, what you want to experience, and how you want to live

---

[47] Jonathan Lockwood Huie, "Spirit Quotes and Sayings: Quotes about Spirit," JonathanLockwoodHuie.com, accessed September 4, 2014, http://www.jonathanlockwoodhuie.com/quotes/spirit/

[48] Eckhart Tolle, *The Power of Now: A Guide to Spiritual Enlightenment* (Vancouver: Namaste Publishing, 1999)

life. Are you just surviving and leading a pretty mundane life? Have you ever had the feeling that you were meant to be doing something else? If you are unhappy with your job and are experiencing anxiety and frustration, it is time for a major life change.

You are probably fulfilling your programmed purpose, which is possibly something that someone else recommended. Perhaps one of your parents encouraged you to be what they are or what they wish they would have been. Your true purpose is what *you* love doing and what you should be doing. Your true purpose (also known as your soul's purpose) is when you are in exact alignment with your highest power and creativity. God will guide you to your true purpose. You have to be willing to take risks, accept the uncertainty, and explore new adventures. Programmed purpose and true purpose can sometimes be the same for some people.

The *Merriam-Webster Dictionary* defines the full definition of *purpose* as *"something set up as an object or end to be attained; a subject under discussion; an action in course of execution; by intent."*[49] A purpose is an intentional act to attain a common end.

What are your personal strengths? What makes you feel spunky? What is your passion? Would you do it for free just for the enjoyment you get from it? Open your mind and your heart to the infinite possibilities. By focusing on your desires and what you can do, one best moment will lead to another best moment, and so on. You must be in total alignment with the present moment and focused on what you are doing instead of what you are thinking. When you are silent, go within, and align your inner being with God. You will discover your purpose in life.

Sometimes we are called by God to contribute our unique gifts and talents to the world. This calling is according to God's will and purpose for our lives. When we put God first, serve God, and live our lives through God, we will get this calling. This is when God uses us

---

[49] *Merriam-Webster.com*, s.v. "purpose," accessed September 24, 2014, http://www.merriam-webster.com/dictionary/purpose

and our special abilities to carry out our true purpose in life. I was compelled to write this book, which I believe was my calling from God.

The first full definition of *calling* by the *Merriam-Webster Dictionary* is *"a strong inner impulse toward a particular course of action especially when accompanied by conviction of divine influence."*[50]

Only you know what is right for you and what you want. No one else knows your life better. Do what makes you happy, use your imagination, and be confident with your choices. Choose something that interests you and keeps your attention. Whatever you decide to do in life, you should do it with acceptance, enthusiasm, and/or enjoyment. When you feel at least one of these three things, you will be much happier. If you have a negative attitude about your job, you should start looking for a new one. Remember, you get to choose what you want to do.

I will be honest with you, there will be obstacles, and yes, you may fail, but stay positive and keep moving forward. You might find out that what you thought you would like, you end up disliking. That is okay. Try something different that attracts your attention. Variety is the spice of life. You may possibly discover skills and abilities you never knew you had. Have faith and keep reminding yourself that you are capable of succeeding. Here is an inspired quote written by Mr. Jerry Dunn to put into practice: *"Don't limit your challenges; challenge your limits."* [51]

When you are doing something you love doing, you are in a more positive and peaceful state, and you will achieve great results. You will be totally focused on the doing, and the events that follow will come naturally to you. My daughter, Chelsea, has the ability to recognize what is beautiful. She used her creative interior decorating ideas and recently remodeled an older house and quickly transformed it into her

---

[50] *Merriam-Webster.com*, s.v. "calling," accessed September 24, 2014, http://www.merriam-webster.com/dictionary/calling

[51] "Jerry Dunn> Quotes> Quotable Quotes," Goodreads.com, accessed on February 3, 2015, https://www.goodreads.com/quotes/245363-don-t-limit-your-challenges-challenge-your-limits

home. Chelsea selected colors and materials for the exterior siding, roofing, and decking, and for the interior walls and flooring. She coordinated furniture, wall décor, carpeting, window treatments, etc., to match. Her clothing, hairstyles, accessories, and shoes, as well as little Liam's (her son) outfits reflect her natural flair for high fashion.

If you are in college, take an elective or a class that is not one of the requirements for your degree. Try something fun such as painting, meditation, pottery, or photography. You might find out that you really like it. Continue to learn something new every day. When you are doing what you love to do with style and purpose and being creative through self-expression, it will be all pleasure. You will be a lot happier because self-expression is a natural part of life. God gave you imaginative and intuitive abilities, so be sure to put them to good use. The world needs your contributions. Here is a famous quote by Mr. Howard Thurman:

> *Don't ask what the world needs;*
> *Ask what makes you come alive.*
> *And go do it.*
> *Because what the world needs is people who have come*
> *alive.*[52]

Intuition

Have you ever had a funny feeling about something? At the beginning of life, we were given a natural instinct to know right from wrong. We were born with an excellent guidance system called intuition, also known as wisdom, instinct, inner voice, spiritual guide, etc. Intuition is the very essence of source which exists within each of us. It is the root of the soul. We did not obtain intuition from education. We got this inner intelligence directly from God.

---

[52] "Howard Thurman > Quotes > Quotable Quote," Goodreads. com, accessed September 24, 2014, http://www.goodreads.com/ quotes/6273-don-t-ask-what-the-world-needs-ask-what-makes-you

Intuition is the subconscious part of you that knows exactly what is right for you. It is good to acquire knowledge and be educated, but it is your intuition that gives you guidance in life that cannot be learned. Usually, when you do something spontaneous, it turns out to be very gratifying and more fun. This instant action comes from an intuitive feeling deep within your being instead of a thought that has been pondered. Intuition provides the guidance you need to fulfill your purpose in life.

Our intuition tells us what to do in any given situation. We usually recognize this when we get older and become more in touch with it. The voices in your head will sometimes give you conflicting messages. Trust and listen to your intuition, and you will know the difference. Your intuition will guide you to make the right choices and put you on the right path. Listen to the positive whispers that come from within.

Do not always let other people's opinions influence your decisions. Some people think they know what is best for us, but it cannot compare to the wisdom that exists within us. If you have a hunch or gut feeling about something, go with it, because it is usually right. Trust your own decision making. Let your instincts be your guide, and do not follow what other people say and do. Their ideas, beliefs, and circumstances may be totally different than yours. Be your own leader. After all, no one knows you better than you. Your intuition is your best guide.

A good example is when you take a test. It is always best to keep the original answer rather than going back and changing it. If you go with your first answer, chances are it is the correct answer. Do not second-guess yourself. When we doubt ourselves, we are not relying on our intuition. There have been times when I did not trust my own judgment. I always wanted a second opinion from others, and oftentimes, I would go along with their ideas. Later, I finally discovered my initial thought would have been the best way to go. This has been a valuable learning experience for me.

Intuition comes naturally at any time, but you can also access it through being silent and still. To get you there, you have to first quiet your mind and thoughts and give up thinking. You have to have faith and trust in your natural powers and abilities. Meditation is an excellent way to gain direct access to your personal power or inspiration within you.

Most importantly, if you follow your heart's desire and let your intuition guide you, you will find your purpose in life. When you get a sudden impulse to do something, take some time to contemplate the effects before proceeding. When in doubt, use your natural wisdom instead of your mind. It is so much more powerful and effective. Connect with your inner guidance system, and your life will be filled with peace and contentment.

Meditation

Do you know what meditation is? Meditation and medication sound alike and both have the same purpose. Both are used for the healing and renewal process of a human being. However, medication is a purchased substance that is absorbed into the body that may cause side effects, while meditation is a natural method accessing the mind, body, and spirit. Meditation is a form of therapy that is perfect for stress management, and it is free.

Meditation is for absolutely everyone. It is the best practice for achieving a higher level of awareness. Meditation is a state in which you transcend the mind and go deeper into reality or consciousness. It is the practice of letting go of any resistance, frustrations, or expectations you may have. Meditation is an excellent way to help you unwind and quiet your mind and thoughts. Did you ever try not to think any thoughts at all? It takes a lot of concentration to block out your thoughts. Through meditation, you learn to deal with your thoughts and become less identified with them. There are no goals or objectives but to just *be* with yourself. Meditation stabilizes the heart rate, improves blood pressure, reduces tension and stress, and gives you peace of mind.

Meditation can be a spiritual practice for connecting your innermost being with God. We all have an individual relationship with the creator of the universe. During meditation, you will develop a greater connection with God. This personal connection is when you receive and accept the will to do the things that are planned for you in order to achieve your purpose in life. This is the ultimate form of spiritual development. Through meditation, you will discover your true self. You will experience a sense of peace and fulfillment in knowing that everything is as it should be.

I strongly urge everyone to learn to meditate. People nowadays are moving at such a fast pace that they seldom take time out for themselves. Try it for at least one week to see if anything happens. You have nothing to lose but so much to gain. See how things are going or if you feel any differently. You can meditate anywhere, but a quiet space is best for concentration. You must commit to regular practice to get positive results. For starters, meditate for at least ten to fifteen minutes a day, and as you become more comfortable with the process, do a little more each day. The more you practice, the easier it will become. I guarantee that you will feel more relaxed and at peace, and you will be able to manage life better.

Find a space and sit comfortably. Relax your entire body until it becomes completely still. Close your eyes to avoid distractions from the outside world. Solely focus on your inner being and breathing. Start by taking a few long, deep breaths in and slowly exhaling. Breathing is an important part of the meditation process. It helps bring you into a more conscious state and takes attention away from our thoughts.

As you meditate, release all the tension and stress and anything that is bothering you. When you start to notice your thoughts, let them come and go like clouds floating by in the sky. Take more deep breaths to bring you back to the awareness state. Conscious breathing during meditation and even throughout the day restores calmness within and helps you to accept and face any new challenges. Breathing is a vital process required to sustain human life.

When you mind starts to wander, bring yourself back to focus on meditating again. When you notice any thoughts or images, change your focus to something such as your breath, your heartbeat, or a word that gives you a warm, fuzzy feeling like *love, joy,* or *peace.* Your thoughts will come and go, and you can ignore them or simply observe them and then let them go. Say to yourself, "Oh, there goes a thought … and there goes another one." Let all your fears, worries, and frustrations fade away, and soon you will become still.

Meditation will help you feel the aliveness throughout your body. Enjoy being in the present moment, and tap into the spirit within you. Here is where you will find all your answers. Keep an open and clear mind. Be quiet and listen to God's voice. When you become aware of your inner being, life force, essence, or whatever you want to label it, you will receive goodness and guidance on how to live according to God's way.

Meditate as often as possible. At first it may be difficult, but as with anything, it takes practice and commitment to achieve great results. Practice as if you are mastering a skill. You will enjoy meditating once you get used to it. Before long, you will be able to meditate anywhere and for maybe just a few minutes, like when you are stuck in traffic, sitting at your desk, lying in bed, sitting on a park bench, waiting on someone, etc. I prefer a quiet space, because it is easier for me to stay focused. I meditate at work when I can, but often there are too many distractions in the office, so I will take a break and go out to my car. I meditate and de-stress for about ten to fifteen minutes. Afterward, I feel renewed and restored and ready to take on my responsibilities. Productivity starts with improvement of the self. It would be more convenient if every place of employment had a room designated for meditation and/or prayer.

You will be amazed at how you will feel and what you will accomplish. The more you meditate, the better you will feel. You will be more energized to handle a busy day and deal with whatever situations arise. If you want to discover your purpose in life, this is a sure way of doing so. God will give you the guidance you are seeking through this process. Be still and let God speak to you. Nothing may happen during meditation or immediately afterward. Be patient and go about your day. I promise you that you will receive the guidance you need. At times when I am meditating, I get emotional and overwhelmed with joy in knowing that I understand life and that I finally have something to believe. This is when I know I am totally aligned with God in a stronger sense than normal.

Meditation and sleep are both excellent ways to relax the mind and body. It is extremely important to give yourself adequate rest mentally and physically. Sleep is a natural state of rest in which your consciousness becomes dormant. Sleep is very comforting, but the minute you wake up, all those thoughts come streaming into your head again one right after another. It is kind of like a Black Friday when all the people are lined up outside the store, waiting to get in. As soon as the doors are opened, the customers rush into the store. So, since we cannot sleep all day long, meditation certainly gives us a calming effect that helps us deal with our thoughts and everyday activities. Meditation also gives us a global connection to all other beings.

I have completed several guided meditation programs offered by many great spiritual teachers. These programs have helped me tremendously with my daily meditation practice. They are available online and are listed below with a brief summary. I strongly encourage you to take some of these courses for further development.

- *"The 21-Day Consciousness Cleanse: A Breakthrough Program for Connecting with Your Soul's Deepest Purpose"* developed by Ms. Debbie Ford. This program was designed to clear the mind and heart from negative thoughts and feelings that build up over time and too often guide decisions and behaviors.
- *"Perfect Health and Miraculous Relationships"* presented by Ms. Oprah Winfrey and Mr. Deepak Chopra. This series

promoted whole wellness for the mind, body, and spirit and expanded the understanding of how to create and live a life filled with authentic true love.

- *"21-Day Mantra Meditation Journey"* with Deva Premal and Miten. This program explored the transformative power of a daily meditation practice and featured twenty-one specially selected mantras with guided meditations that supported well-being and a deeper state of inner peace.

- *"21 Days of Gratitude"* presented by award winning cinematographer Mr. Louie Schwartzberg. Mr. Schwartzberg guided the meditations and twenty-one pre-eminent mentors provided inspirational thoughts to enhance every aspect of life with gratitude.

- *"21-Day Meditation Experience—Desire and Destiny"* offered by Ms. Oprah Winfrey and Mr. Deepak Chopra. This transformational three-week journey provided guidance on living with passion and abundance, uncovering creative brilliance, connecting with deep desires, and tapping into pure potential.

- *"21 Meditations on Love"* by Ms. Janet Bray Attwood. This journey connected the mind, body, and spirit to love in ways to allow us to fully appreciate this divine gift we all have access to, but few truly experience in its fullness.

- *"21-Day Meditation Experience—Finding Your Flow."* Ms. Oprah Winfrey and Mr. Deepak Chopra team up again to reveal the secrets to finding flow and to leverage its mighty power to joy, love, and fulfillment.

- *"Osho - A Course in Meditation – 21 Day Workout for your Consciousness."* The words you hear from World renowned, contemporary mystic Osho are intended to get your attention, heighten all your senses and show you the value of using your whole being - spirit, mind and body, to reach new spiritual heights.

- *"21-Day Meditation Experience – Expanding Your Happiness."* During the three weeks, Ms. Oprah Winfrey and Mr. Deepak Chopra teach us that happiness is much more than an aspiration. Happiness is our true nature – our very source of being, and when we expand our awareness within, we discover that there is no limit to our happiness.

Prayer

Do you pray? Prayer and meditation are similar in that you are connecting with God. When you pray, you are speaking to God. Typically you are asking for something, or you may be thanking God for all your blessings. Meditation is when you are simply listening for divine guidance from God as we discussed in the above section. Do you call upon God to give you guidance in your life? Do you let God guide the way when you are making difficult decisions? When you ask, you shall receive. You would not believe how much less stressful your life would be if you connect with God and let God do the work.

You can pray anywhere, anytime. You can go to any place of worship to pray, or you can even pray at home. Many people get discouraged when they believe their prayers go unanswered. I would like to explain this for you. First, you have got to believe and have faith that God will answer your prayers. Your prayers will be answered in one of three approaches: yes, not yet, or there is something better. Be patient, because it might not happen right away. If you do not get what you have been praying for, then God must have a better plan in store for you. Constantly begging God to answer a prayer indicates lack of faith. It will take longer when you keep asking. You only have to ask one time.

Thoughts and prayers are very powerful, and when many people are on the same high energy level, great things happen. Prayer has the power to heal and transform our lives. When you pray for others, they will pray for you. When people come together to form a collective and pray together, everyone is on the same high frequency, sending positive energy and intention out to the universe. The results are amazing. This is when miracles happen. Imagine what we could accomplish if there were large groups of people praying for the same thing. Diseases, cancer, and illnesses are known to be cured. Life experiences are meant to be shared, good and bad. Visit this website: Helpguide.org @ http://www.helpguide.org/life/spirituality_prayers. htm for inspiration. It is a trusted non-profit resource that offers prayers for strength, healing, and coping with life's challenges. Pray to God, because God is listening.

Peace and Harmony

I wonder what it would be like if there were no more wars or hostility in this world and only peace and harmony existed. Can you imagine everyone getting along? Mr. A. J. Muste wrote a statement in 1967 about peace, "*There is no way to* peace*; peace is the way,*"[53] although this statement has also became widely attributed to Mr. Mahatma Gandhi. Well, if we want to live in a more peaceful world, we have to begin by creating peace within ourselves. Peace is of the mind and in the heart. Peace is being satisfied with ourselves and what is. Peace is having true faith. In order to achieve inner peace, always accept the present moment for what it is without wishing it was something else. Go with the flow of life and keep your thoughts and emotions in check. Move forward in life with a positive attitude, and be understanding and forgiving.

When you do not react to drama, and accept every precious moment as it is, you will have inner peace and contentment. Of course, it is only natural to be sad when tragedy strikes or when certain situations occur, such as the loss of a loved one or a pet, etc. But you will be able to handle these difficult life situations in a practical manner. You should still let your emotions flow freely when you experience grief and sorrow, knowing you will have great

---

[53] "A.J. Muste," Wikiquote, last modified January 8, 2015, http://en.wikiquote.org/wiki/A._J._Muste

healing. This inner peace will keep your life balanced and your emotions under control.

Growing up as a child, I did not like conflict and always tried to be the peacemaker in the family, just like my father. My father was a typical family man and was very passive. He avoided social gatherings and simply preferred to stay at home. Today, I avoid conflict if at all possible. Situations do indeed require attention so that issues can be resolved. You can resolve them in a peaceful manner, as long as you have peace within you.

When we constantly to do the right thing, eventually people will take notice and want to do the same. One person's energy is very powerful and transmittable. Can you imagine what it would be like if we all came together with an enormous amount of positive energy to help and support each other, especially the people who are experiencing pain and powerlessness in their lives? You could smile to yourself, knowing that you affected the world with your love and encouragement.

To have peace in the world, peace must begin within each one of us. Here is a wonderful quote by Chinese philosopher Mr. Lao Tzu I would like to share with you:

> *"If there is to be peace in the world,*
> *There must be peace in the nations.*
> *If there is to be peace in the nations,*
> *There must be peace in the cities.*
> *If there is to be peace in the cities,*
> *There must be peace between neighbors.*
> *If there is to be peace between neighbors,*
> *There must be peace in the home.*
> *If there is to be peace in the home,*
> *There must be peace in the heart."*[54]

---

[54] "Lao Tzu > Quotes > Quotable Quote," Goodreads.com, accessed August 14, 2014, http://www.goodreads.com/quotes/125184-if-there-is-to-be-peace-in-the-world-there

CHAPTER 14

Staying in the Moment

Past

Why are we so addicted to the past? Are you living in the past? Do you regret things you have done, should have done, or even wish you would have done differently? We have made choices in the past and some were good and some were not the best, but that is all part of life's journey. The past is gone forever so why dwell on it? You must quit reliving the past and stop playing the victim. You are creating useless pain and suffering for yourself. Cherish the good memories and move on. Put the past behind you and begin to take control of your life.

When you keep letting your mind go back to the past and think about what you regret, or who offended you, etc., you are focusing on events that have already happened that you have no control over. You are not in the now, and you may be missing out on something extraordinary like a sign from God to help you make a critical decision. You could miss seeing someone you have been waiting to see. You might miss hearing something that could change your entire day or outlook on life.

Here is the perfect quote for this topic. It is written by Bishop T. D. Jakes:

> *When you hold on to*
> *your history, you do*

141

> *it at the expense of*
> *your destiny.*[55]

Your past has passed. It is history. It is a done deal. There is nothing you can do about it. Excuse me; yes, there is something you can do ... and that is to forget about it!

Believe it or not, there was something good that came from those negative experiences. Those types of things were meant to happen perhaps to help grow from them. When you look at the big picture, it could have been a lesson you needed to learn. Certain things need to happen in order for other events to occur. If you still do not understand, you may just want to forget about the negative things that happened.

We should not totally forget the past. By all means, remember the good times you had and the wonderful people you met. However, wishing for the way things used to be can cause sadness. Focus on what is happening in your life right now. If you are unhappy, you have the opportunity to change things. Pay close attention to every feeling you have and everything you do in every moment of every day, because this is when you make better choices. Ultimately, being in the present moment is when you have your chance to change your life.

Future

Do you stress about the future and what *might* happen? Earlier in this book, I talked about fear and worry. Remember, we have no control over other people or future events, so why do we worry? We do not know what the future holds for us, so we should be paying attention to what is currently happening in our lives. What good does it do to worry about an event that has not and might not ever occur? You are wasting valuable time.

---

[55]   "Quotables," Oprah.com, accessed September 25, 2014, http://www.oprah.com/quote/Quotes-About-Moving-Forward-Bishop-TD-Jake_1

Have you ever worried yourself silly about something, and everything ended up being perfectly fine or perhaps even better than you thought? You worried for nothing, and as I said before, worrying affects you physically and mentally. You will not be happy when you are constantly worrying!

Yes, you can plan and prepare for the future by going to college to gain more knowledge, get a better job, and be more independent. You can put some money aside for a vacation, a new car, or whatever, but you must not live for the future. You have to be happy now and enjoy life. People who live for the future may be missing out on what is currently happening in their lives that could lead to a brighter future.

The joy of life is in the journey, and when you are focused on some future outcome, you will not enjoy the things along the way. Make peace with where you are right now in your life's journey instead of being concerned about the end result.

Living in the present moment is the only way to be. Focus on what is happening right now at this very moment and enjoy every minute of it. Keep the faith and know that everything will work out. Know that you do not have to worry about a thing you do not have control over anyhow. When you let your inner being guide you, you will live your life to the fullest! You deserve nothing but the best, so just sit back and enjoy the ride!

Present Moment

Are you living life in the present moment … right here … right now? This is the very last subject I am going to talk about, because it is the most important. Being in the present moment means to be conscious and completely focused on what you are doing and all that is going on around you. When you stay in the present moment, you will make wiser choices that will empower you to create the life you want.

The present moment is what you are doing this very second (like reading *Break Free From Your Reins*). Are you absorbing what you are reading, or are your thoughts all over the place? Are you thinking about what you are going to do tonight, where you are going, and who you are going with? Are you aware of what your thoughts are right now? If you are, you are definitely making progress. Are you aware of the presence of God in each and every moment? Present moment awareness is essential if we wish to evolve as human beings.

Everything you do in life should be done in the present moment and with awareness of God's presence. The more we stay focused on the actual *doing* and *believing* as opposed to our thoughts, the more we will experience joy and fulfillment as spiritual beings. There may be times when you slip out of the present moment and go back to the past or think about the future. You return to your old habits and thought patterns. No problem, just bring yourself back to the *doing* instead of the thinking. I have heard so many people say they wish they knew back then what they know now. Now is here, and it is your chance to shine. This is your opportunity to make your life amazing.

Do you appreciate this very moment even when you are experiencing difficulties? When things are not going your way, the present moment is not an obstacle to overcome in order to get to another place. When you consider the present moment as an obstacle, you are resisting what is currently happening. You cannot ignore it, but you can change your thoughts about it. You must realize that it is only a temporary situation and that *this too shall pass*. God is in the process of teaching you and/or someone else something about life, and it has to happen in this order to make things right. Trust this process because it is perfect. By being in the present moment and understanding and accepting conditions as they are instead of resisting what is, you will achieve inner peace.

You should also be aware of the people around you and be conscious of their actions. If we are unconscious, we may absorb negative energy. By being present, you will know how to interact with people and handle negative behavior. You will not be tempted to fall into the same pattern and enable their behavior. When people are facing problems or issues, oftentimes they are not in the present moment. They are too caught up with complaining and worrying about the issue, and they do not realize it is interfering with their awareness and attentiveness. However, if you stay focused in the present moment, you will be able to help them by reacting to their issues in a positive manner and providing constructive feedback. This is the best thing you can do for any relationship under any circumstances.

When you want to be there for whomever, you must be in the present moment yourself; otherwise, how can you help anybody if *you* are not there yourself? Remember, there are many people in this world who are not where you are today in life. They are still living in the past or worrying about the future, and negative people can easily change your mood. Do not let their negative thinking affect you. You have the choice to focus on positive thoughts, or you could choose to follow their negative path. In order to make the better choice, you have to be in the present moment, and you will be able to resolve issues in a more peaceful and loving manner.

Make the present moment the primary focus of your life. Do not wish to be any place (past or future) but where you are right now. Enjoy and be grateful for the present moment. It is very important to constantly stay focused and be aware of what you are thinking, what you are doing, and what you are saying in every moment. The key to making the right choice at the right time is to be in the present moment and to be aware of what your intuition is telling you. You will know which thoughts to believe and which ones to ignore, and you will make good choices. When you consistently do what is right, you will always be rewarded. God will give you more than you could ever imagine.

Bring consciousness into everything you do and find joy in every second, every minute, every hour, every day, every week, every month, every year, every decade, every century, every millennium, etc., no matter where you are in your life right now. Now do you get it? I encourage you to stay focused in the present moment, even if it is not exactly what you are wanting. When you practice this, you will discover that whatever you are currently experiencing is filled with new energy and is not so bad after all. People will notice your positive approach and hopefully will want to follow your lead. You will eventually be guided to fulfill your purpose in life. Mr. Eckhart Tolle lives his life in the present moment. He wrote some excellent books on the present moment that I highly recommend reading. Check the back of this book for more information.

One time I was asked this question: If I had a chance to change anything in my life, past or present, what would it be? My answer to that question was that I would not change a thing. All the people who have crossed my path and all the events and situations that have occurred in my life have brought me to where I am today. At this very present moment, I know myself better than I ever have, and I am happy and at peace with myself. I will continue to grow into a higher consciousness and be of service to others. The following quote applies to the present moment. According to BrainyQuote.com, it was written by Mr. Babatunde Olatunji:

> *"Yesterday is history,*
> *tomorrow is a mystery.*
> *Today is a gift.*
> *That is why it is called Present."*[56]

---

[56] BrainyQuote.com, accessed September 8, 2014, http://www.brainyquote.com/quotes/quotes/b/babatundeo311872.html

CHAPTER 15

Applying the Knowledge

At this point in your life, you have acquired and absorbed much information. To gain knowledge and experience, you must apply this information to whatever action you are taking. What good is knowing without doing? It does not matter how smart you are or what you know. You can go to school for years, read tons of books, and take many classes, but you have to know what to do with the information you have collected in order to be successful. Learning something new without application is useless.

I sincerely appreciate your taking the time to read *Break Free From Your Reins*. It is a great first step toward transforming your life. It is time to start practicing these principles. When you successfully apply them to your everyday activities, you will soon discover how fantastic life can be. If you do not use it, you will lose it. Stay fully awake, mindful, aware, and conscious to fully embrace life. I absolutely love this next quote. It is my all-time favorite and pretty much sums everything up perfectly. Several individuals have been credited for different versions of this quote; however, according to QuoteInvestigator.com, Mr. Frank Outlaw, the late President of the Bi-Lo store chain, was the earliest author of this one:

> *"Watch your thoughts; they become words.*
> *Watch your words; they become actions.*

> *Watch your actions; they become habits.*
> *Watch your habits; they become character.*
> *Watch your character; for it becomes your destiny.*"[57]

Remember to remember these words in every waking moment. Something interesting to note is when five of the key words are arranged in this order: words, actions, thoughts, character, and habits, the first initial of each word spells w.a.t.c.h.

Every decision you have ever made has brought you to this point in life. You survived, and you are fine. All of your experiences have made you who you are today. Maybe it is time to write a new story. You are the author, so make it a good one! You have great potential, and the truth is, you are *awesome*! I know all your hopes and dreams will take you to where you want to go. As famous philosopher Confucius said, "*Wherever you go, go with all your heart.*"[58]

I wish you much *love, happiness,* and inner *peace* always on your spiritual journey of life. If I could convince you to do one positive thing in life, it would be this: *be* the *best* person you can be. You will contribute to healing this world. What is holding you back? Break free from your reins!

---

[57] QuoteInvestigator.com, accessed September 8, 2014, http://quoteinvestigator.com/2013/01/10/watch-your-thoughts/

[58] BrainyQuote.com, accessed February 3, 2015, http://www.brainyquote.com/quotes/quotes/c/confucius161594.html

I am wide awake.

++++

Thank you, God, for all of life.

++++

All is good with this world and the universe.

++++

I love you, God.

 # About the Author

Author Deborah M. Parise says it is time to praise and celebrate life! She wants everyone to realize how incredibly blessed we are to be alive and that life is really good!

Ms. Parise is originally from the Pittsburgh, Pennsylvania area but currently resides in Fairmont, West Virginia. She has two lovely daughters, Chelsea and Sarah Schwoeble, and an adorable little Maltese named Oscar. Ms. Parise, also known as "Grammie," has been blessed with a handsome grandson named Liam. Liam is the apple of her eye. Ms. Parise is permanently employed full-time and holds the title of Certified Configuration Management Professional. She achieved Level III Certification from the Configuration Training Foundation of the International Society of Configuration Management.

Ms. Parise has learned well from her sixty years of actual life experiences. Her wisdom and intuition, along with the guidance and driving energy force from a divine influence prompted her to write *Break Free From Your Reins*. Ms. Parise's spiritual encounter at her home has been a fulfilling promise (see her personal testimony).

Ms. Parise has been inspired by so many wonderful motivational teachers and spiritual leaders. She finds pleasure in reading books, and for the past several years, the main topic of her interest has been spirituality, positivity, and the law of attraction. She practices and encourages everyone to meditate on a daily basis. She has developed a website to share with the world her positive inspirational messages.

Please visit Ms. Parise's website *Attracting Positive Energy* at: http://www.deborahparise.com/.

Ms. Parise has been devoted to serving others. Her divine purpose in life is to provide guidance and motivation to people on ways to reach their fullest potential and be happy. Ms. Parise knows that if she can help people view themselves in a more positive and confident light, they will grow beyond measure. She offers advice on life in general and how to achieve inner peace. Ms. Parise strongly encourages all people to become the extraordinary individuals they were created to be.

Works Cited

1   BrainyQuote.com, accessed August 14, 2014, http://www.brainyquote.com/quotes/quotes/j/johndrock119902.html

2   BrainyQuote.com, accessed August 14, 2014, http://www.brainyquote.com/quotes/quotes/a/arthurrubi104208.html

3   Kahlil Gibran, *The Prophet,* the section on children, Juan Cole's personal website, accessed June 12, 2014, http://www-personal.umich.edu/~jrcole/gibran/prophet/prophet.htm

4   *Wikipedia,* s.v. "Deity," last modified June 5, 2014, http://en.wikipedia.org/wiki/Diety

5   *Wikipedia,* s.v. "Atheism," last modified June 6, 2014, http://en.wikipedia.org/wiki/Atheism

6   *Wikipedia,* s.v. "Bible," last modified June 7, 2014, http://en.wikipedia.org/wiki/Bible

7   "Rick Warren > Quotes > Quotable Quote," Goodreads.com, accessed August 15, 2014, https://www.goodreads.com/quotes/419680-happy-moments-praise-god-difficult-moments-seek-god-quiet-moments

8   *Wikipedia,* s.v. "Spirituality," last modified June 5, 2014, http://en.wikipedia.org/wiki/Spirituality

9   *Dictionary.com,* s.v. "miracle," accessed June 12, 2014, http://dictionary.reference.com/browse/miracle?s=t&path=/

10 "Mom's hug revives baby that was pronounced dead," Today Parenting, accessed June 12, 2014, http://today.msnbc.

msn.com/id/38988444/ns/today-parenting_and_family/t/
moms-hug-revives-baby-was-pronounced-dead/

[11] "Albert Einstein > Quotes > Quotable Quote," Goodreads.
com, accessed August 15, 2014, http://www.goodreads.com/
quotes/987-there-are-only-two-ways-to-live-your-life-one

[12] "Law of attraction," rationalwiki.org, last modified August 1,
2014, http://rationalwiki.org/wiki/Law_of_attraction

[13] Dictionary.com, s.v. "ego," accessed June 12, 2014, http://
dictionary.reference.com/browse/ego?s=t&path=/

[14] "It's All About Gratitude," TheSecretProgram.com, accessed
August 14, 2014, http://thesecretprogram.com

[15] BrainyQuote.com, accessed August 15, 2014, http://www.
brainyquote.com/quotes/quotes/e/elizabethk100902.html

[16] "Marianne Williamson > Quotes," Goodreads.com, accessed
September 24, 2014, http://www.goodreads.com/author/
quotes/17297.Marianne_Williamson

[17] Terry Cole-Whittaker, *What You Think of Me is None of My
Business*" First published 1979 by Oak Tree Publications, San
Diego, CA.

[18] Oprah Winfrey, "Oprah Shares How to Choose Happiness,"
The Oprah Magazine South Africa, February 2014, http://
www.oprahmag.co.za/live-your-best-life/self-development/
oprah-shares-how-to-choose-happiness

[19] Values.com, accessed August 19, 2014, http://www.values.com/
inspirational-quotes/3687-Hatred-Paralyzes-Life-Love-

[20] Dictionary.com, s.v. "conceited," accessed August 18, 2014,
http://dictionary.reference.com/browse/conceited?s=t

[21] Dictionary.com, s.v. "narcissism," accessed August 18, 2014,
http://dictionary.reference.com/browse/narcissism?s=t

[22] Urban Dictionary.com, last modified January 30,
2004, http://www.urbandictionary.com/define.
php?term=love&defid=480188

[23] Author unknown

[24] BrainyQuote.com, accessed August 29, 2014, http://www.brainyquote.com/quotes/quotes/z/zigziglar381975.html

[25] Author unknown

[26] Values.com, accessed August 19, 2014, http://www.values.com/inspirational-quotes/3130?page=39

[27] "The Beatles Lyrics: 'Let it Be,'" ABC Lyrics, accessed August 29, 2014, http://www.azlyrics.com/lyrics/beatles/letitbe.html

[28] Jack Kornfield, "Did I Love Well," excerpt of *A Path with Heart—A Guide Through the Perils and Promises of Spiritual Life*, accessed August 29, 2014, http://www.yin4men.com/files/59265197c5c5c28b45e5f3b50eeccc2f-143.html

[29] "Thích Nhất Hạnh > Quotes > Quotable Quote," Goodreads.com, accessed September 25, 2014, https://www.goodreads.com/quotes/350914-to-be-beautiful-means-to-be-yourself-you-don-t-need

[30] "Creating a New Earth Together," Oprah talks to Eckhart Tolle, by Oprah, O Magazine, Paragraph 13, eckharttolle.com, accessed January 30, 2015, http://www.eckharttolle.com/article/Eckhart-Tolle-Oprah-Winfrey-O-Magazine-Interview

[31] *The Wisdom of Making the Right Choices*, Joyce Meyer Ministries, accessed September 25, 2014, https://www.joycemeyer.org/Content/Downloads/bootcamp_the_wisdom_of_making_right_choices.pdf

[32] "Frank Abagnale Jr.," A&E Television Networks, accessed July 30, 2014, http://www.biography.com/#!/people/frank-abagnale-20657335

[33] Neil Gaiman, inspirational commencement speech at the University of the Arts, 2012

[34] "Helen Keller > Quotes > Quotable Quotes," Goodreads.com, accessed September 15, 2014, http://www.goodreads.com/quotes/4900-the-best-and-most-beautiful-things-in-the-world-cannot

35 Robert A. Schuller and Douglas Di Siena, *Possibility Living: Add Years to Your Life and Life to Your Years with God's Health Plan* (New York: HarperOne, 2002)

36 "Spirituality Practice, Resources for Spiritual Journeys," Spiritualityandpractice.com, An Excerpt from Courage: *Overcoming Fear and Igniting Self-Confidence* by Debbie Ford, accessed February 3, 2015, http://www.spiritualityandpractice. com/books/excerpts.php?id=22716

37 "Enchanted Love Quotes," Goodreads.com, accessed September, 17, 2014, https://www.goodreads.com/work/quotes/398021-enchanted-love-the-mystical-power-of-intimate-relationships

38 BrainyQuote.com, accessed September 17, 2014, http://www. brainyquote.com/quotes/quotes/b/benjaminfr103731.html

39 Author unknown

40 "When You Learn to Accept," livelifehappy.com, accessed September 17, 2014, http://www.livelifehappy. com/?s=robert+fisher

41 "Joseph Addison > Quotes > Quotable Quote," Goodreads. com, accessed August 15, 2014, http://www.goodreads.com/ quotes/76178-what-sunshine-is-to-flowers-smiles-are-to-humanity-these

42 BrainyQuote.com, accessed August 15, 2014, http://www. brainyquote.com/quotes/quotes/g/georgebern120971.html

43 *Wikipedia*, s.v. "Jack of all trades, master of none," last modified August 31, 2014, http://en.wikipedia.org/wiki/ Jack_of_all_trades,_master_of_none

44 "The Wisdom of Eckhart Tolle," Peaceful Rivers, accessed September 18, 2014, http://peacefulrivers.homestead.com/ EckhartTolle.html

45 "Book Review," Spirituality and Practice, accessed September 25, 2014, http://www.spiritualityandpractice.com/books/books. php?id=18576

46 Author unknown

[47] Jonathan Lockwood Huie, "Spirit Quotes and Sayings: Quotes about Spirit," JonathanLockwoodHuie.com, accessed September 4, 2014, http://www.jonathanlockwoodhuie.com/quotes/spirit/

[48] Eckhart Tolle, *The Power of Now: A Guide to Spiritual Enlightenment* (Vancouver: Namaste Publishing, 1999)

[49] *Merriam-Webster.com*, s.v. "purpose," accessed September 24, 2014, http://www.merriam-webster.com/dictionary/purpose

[50] *Merriam-Webster.com*, s.v. "calling," accessed September 24, 2014, http://www.merriam-webster.com/dictionary/calling

[51] "Jerry Dunn> Quotes> Quotable Quotes," Goodreads.com, accessed on February 3, 2015, https://www.goodreads.com/quotes/245363-don-t-limit-your-challenges-challenge-your-limits

[52] "Howard Thurman > Quotes > Quotable Quote," Goodreads.com, accessed September 24, 2014, http://www.goodreads.com/quotes/6273-don-t-ask-what-the-world-needs-ask-what-makes-you

[53] "A.J. Muste," Wikiquote, last modified June 7, 2014, http://en.wikiquote.org/wiki/A. J. Muste

[54] "Lao Tzu > Quotes > Quotable Quote," Goodreads.com, accessed August 14, 2014, http://www.goodreads.com/quotes/125184-if-there-is-to-be-peace-in-the-world-there

[55] "Quotables," Oprah.com, accessed September 25, 2014, http://www.oprah.com/quote/Quotes-About-Moving-Forward-Bishop-TD-Jake_1

[56] BrainyQuote.com, accessed September 8, 2014, http://www.brainyquote.com/quotes/quotes/b/babatundeo311872.html

[57] QuoteInvestigator.com, accessed September 8, 2014, http://quoteinvestigator.com/2013/01/10/watch-your-thoughts/

[58] BrainyQuote.com, accessed February 3, 2015, http://www.brainyquote.com/quotes/quotes/c/confucius161594.html

Recommended Reading

I have shared a list of sources below that I have found to be very effective in providing key spiritual principles for improving my life. All of these authors have inspired me in some way. If you truly want to understand yourself and live a more meaningful life, I encourage you to read some of these books. Be bold, be brave, and be better!

A New Earth Awakening to Your Life's Purpose by Eckhart Tolle
Broken Open by Elizabeth Lesser
Daily O—Nurturing Mind, Body & Spirit (http://www.dailyom.com/)
Happy for No Reason by Marci Shimoff
Loving What Is by Byron Katie and Stephen Mitchell
New Day New You by Joyce Meyer
Oneness With All Life by Eckhart Tolle
Stillness Speaks by Eckhart Tolle
The Age of Miracles by Marianne Williamson
The Power of Now by Eckhart Tolle
The Seat of the Soul by Gary Zukav
The Secret by Rhonda Byrne
The Seeker's Guide by Elizabeth Lesser
Wherever You Go There You Are by Jon Kabat-Zinn
Your Best Life Now by Joel Osteen

Online Resources

No matter what problems you are facing in life, you do not need to do it alone. There are ways to get help, but you have to decide for yourself. Reach out to someone and let him or her know your situation. There are so many highly qualified, trained professionals who care and will provide the support you need and help guide you in the right direction. To get started, please take advantage of the resources provided below. You will soon be back on track. Life is definitely worth living!

- About Opioid Dependence, Turn to Help (http://turntohelp.com/?utm_campaign=suboxone_incremental_FY2012&utm_medium=banner&utm_source=aol&utm_content=aol&utm_term=91852493_orange_unbranded_cpa_300x250)
- American Foundation for Suicide Prevention (http://www.afsp.org/understanding-suicide)
- Age of Consent/Wikipedia (http://en.wikipedia.org/wiki/Ages_of_consent)
- Alcoholics Anonymous (http://www.aa.org/)
- Childhelp National Child Abuse Hotline (http://www.childhelp.org/pages/hotline-home)
- Family Matters Resource Center (http://www.familymatterscares.org/)

- Kids Health/Helping Kids Deal with Bullies (http://kids health.org/parent/emotions/behavior/bullies.html)
- Legal Drinking Age/Wikipedia (http://en.wikipedia.org/ wiki/Legal_drinking_age)
- National Suicide Prevention Lifeline (http://www. suicidepreventionlifeline.org)
  24-Hour National Suicide Prevention Helpline: 1-800-273-TALK (8255)
- The National Center for Victims of Crime (http://www. ncvc.org/)